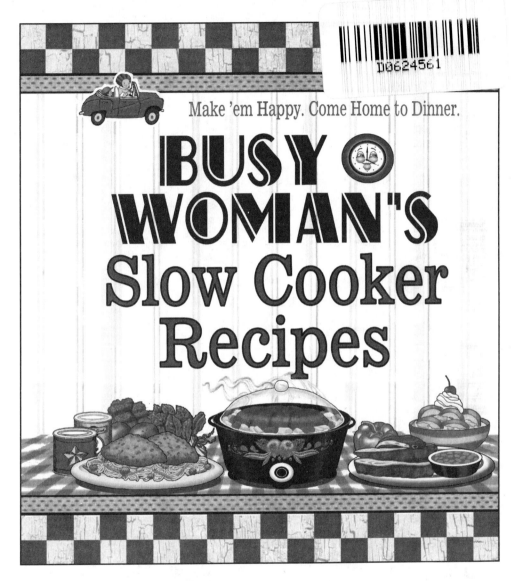

Make 'em Happy. Come Home to Dinner.

BUSY WOMAN'S Slow Cooker Recipes

Cookbook Resources LLC
Highland Village, Texas

Busy Woman's Slow Cooker Recipes
Make "em Happy. Come Home to Dinner.

1st Printing - April 2007
2nd Printing - November 2007
3rd Printing - March 2008
4th Printing - October 2008
5th Printing - November 2008
6th Printing - April 2009
7th Printing - October 2009

International Standard Book Number: 978-1-59769-035-5

Library of Congress Control Number: 2008935586

Library of Congress Cataloging-in-Publication Data

Cover and Illustrations by Nancy Bohanan

Edited, Designed and Published in the United States of America by
Cookbook Resources, LLC
541 Doubletree Drive
Highland Village, Texas 75077

Toll free 866-229-2665

www.cookbookresources.com

Bringing Family and Friends to the Table

Busy Woman's Slow Cooker Recipes

B usy women need help. That's right. Multi-tasking doesn't hold a candle to all the things busy women do in any given day. That's why the *Busy Woman's Slow Cooker Recipes* cookbook is made just for someone who needs to simplify and to harmonize.

Simple meals bring harmony to all who take part. Meals are greatly underrated by most of us and the experts tell us why they are so important.

Children in families that regularly share mealtimes together are more likely to make good grades in school than those who don't share meals with their families.

Children who enjoy the safety, security and comfort of family meals are more likely to stay out of trouble and less likely to drink, smoke or do drugs than those who don't share meals with their families.

And, the best place for children to learn family values, sharing and building relationships is around the family dinner table. The best place for children to grow up is around the dinner table with their families.

Busy women make time for family and friends and cook the comforting and reassuring meals most of us take for granted. Busy women know what's important and busy women can make it all happen.

To all the busy women who take time to prepare meals, we salute you and hope that *Busy Woman's Slow Cooker Recipes* will make your life a little easier.

Contents

Contents

Dedication

With a mission of helping you bring family and friends to the table, Cookbook Resources strives to make family meals and entertaining friends simple, easy and delicious.

We recognize the importance of a meal together as a means of building family bonds with memories and traditions that will be treasured for a lifetime. It is an opportunity to sit down with each other and share more than food.

This cookbook is dedicated with gratitude and respect for all those who show their love with homecooked meals, bringing family and friends to the table.

More and more statistical studies are finding that family meals play a significant role in childhood development. Children who eat with their families four or more nights per week are healthier, make better grades, score higher on aptitude tests and are less likely to have problems with drugs.

Appetizers
Snacks, Wings,
Spreads, Dips

Appetizers Contents

*Always read the entire recipe before you begin
preparing food for the slow cooker or any recipe.*

Bourbon Dogs

1 (1 pound) package wieners	455 g
½ cup chili sauce	135 g
⅔ cup packed brown sugar	150 g
½ cup bourbon	125 ml

- Cut wieners diagonally into bite-size pieces.

- Combine chili sauce, brown sugar and bourbon in sprayed, small slow cooker.

- Stir in wieners and cook on LOW for 1 to 2 hours.

- Serve in chafing dish. Serves 4.

Cocktail Franks

These little guys pack quite a punch.

1 cup packed brown sugar	220 g
1 cup chili sauce	270 g
1 tablespoon red wine vinegar	15 ml
2 teaspoons soy sauce	10 ml
2 teaspoons dijon-style mustard	10 ml
2 (12 ounce) packages frankfurters	2 (340 g)

- Combine brown sugar, chili sauce, vinegar, soy sauce and mustard in sprayed, small slow cooker and mix well. Cut frankfurters diagonally in 1-inch (2.5 cm) pieces. Stir in frankfurters.

- Cover and cook on LOW for 1 to 2 hours.

- Serve from cooker using cocktail picks. Serves 8.

Honey I Ate All the Wings

1 (2 pound) package chicken wingettes	910 g
2 cups honey	680 g
¾ cup soy sauce	175 ml
¾ cup chili sauce	205 g
¼ cup oil	60 ml
1 teaspoon minced garlic	5 ml
Dried parsley flakes, optional	

- Rinse chicken, pat dry and sprinkle with a little salt and pepper.

- Place wingettes in broiler pan and broil for 20 minutes (10 minutes on each side) or until light brown.

- Transfer to sprayed slow cooker.

- Combine honey, soy sauce, chili sauce, oil and garlic in bowl and spoon over wingettes.

- Cover and cook on LOW for 4 to 5 hours or on HIGH for 2 hours to 2 hours 30 minutes. Garnish with dried parsley flakes if desired. Serves 8 to 10.

No-Burn Chicken Wings

Great for the kids!

2½ pounds chicken wingettes   1.1 kg
1 onion, chopped
1 cup soy sauce   250 ml
1 cup packed brown sugar   220 g
1 teaspoon minced garlic   5 ml
1½ teaspoons ground ginger   7 ml

- Rinse chicken and pat dry. Place chicken wingettes in broiler pan and broil about 10 minutes on both sides.

- Transfer wingettes to sprayed, large slow cooker.

- Combine onion, soy sauce, brown sugar, garlic and ginger in bowl. Spoon sauce over wingettes.

- Cook on HIGH for 2 hours. Stir wingettes once during cooking to coat chicken evenly with sauce. Serves 8 to 10.

Ol' Smokies

1 cup ketchup	270 g
1 cup plum jelly	320 g
1 tablespoon lemon juice	15 ml
2 (5 ounce) packages tiny smoked sausages	2 (145 g)

- Combine all ingredients in sprayed, small slow cooker.

- Cover and cook on LOW for 1 hour.

- Stir before serving. Serve right from cooker. Serves 4 to 6.

Sweet Sausage Bites

The pineapple tames the kick of the sausage.

1 (1 pound) link cooked Polish sausage, skinned	455 g
1 (1 pound) hot bulk sausage	455 g
1 (8 ounce) can crushed pineapple with juice	230 g
1 cup apricot preserves	320 g
1 tablespoon marinade for chicken	15 ml
1½ cups packed brown sugar	330 g

- Slice link sausage into ½-inch (1.2 cm) pieces. Shape bulk sausage into 1-inch (2.5 cm) balls and brown in skillet.

- Place sausage pieces, sausage balls, pineapple, apricot preserves, marinade for chicken and brown sugar in sprayed slow cooker. Stir gently so meatballs do not break up.

- Cover and cook on LOW for 1 hour 30 minutes to 2 hours. Serves 8 to 10.

Arti-Crab Crisps

Artichoke and crab are a delicious, classic combination.

1 (6 ounce) can crabmeat, flaked	170 g
½ cup grated parmesan cheese	50 g
1 bunch fresh green onions, sliced	
1½ tablespoons lemon juice	22 ml
1 (15 ounce) can artichoke hearts, drained, finely chopped	425 g
1 (8 ounce) package cream cheese, cubed	230 g
Toasted bagel chips	

- Combine all ingredients in sprayed, small slow cooker and stir well.

- Cover and cook on LOW for 1 hour to 1 hour 30 minutes. Stir until cream cheese mixes well.

- Serve on toasted bagel chips. Serves 4 to 6.

Oktoberfest Spread

1 (8 ounce) package shredded Swiss cheese	230 g
¾ cup drained sauerkraut, rinsed, drained	110 g
1 (8 ounce) package cream cheese, softened, cubed	230 g
2 (2.5 ounce) packages sliced corned beef, chopped	2 (70 g)
Rye bread	

- Combine Swiss cheese, sauerkraut, cream cheese and corned beef in bowl and spoon into sprayed, small slow cooker.

- Cover and cook on LOW for 1 hour.

- Serve on slices of 3-inch (8 cm) rye bread. Serves 4 to 6.

Fiery Sausage Dip

1 pound hot sausage	455 g
1 (10 ounce) can diced tomatoes and green chilies	280 g
1 (2 pound) box Velveeta® cheese	910 g

- Brown and cook sausage in skillet, drain and place in sprayed, small slow cooker.

- Stir in tomatoes and green chilies and mix well. Cut cheese into chunks and add to sausage-tomato mixture.

- Cover and cook on LOW for 1 hour or until cheese melts.

- Stir when ready to serve and serve hot in slow cooker. Serves 4 to 6.

TIP: This works best with large tortilla chips.

Chili-Cheese Dip

2 (15 ounce) cans chili	2 (425 g)
1 (10 ounce) can diced tomatoes and green chilies	280 g
1 (16 ounce) package cubed Velveeta® cheese	455 g
1 bunch fresh green onions, chopped	

- Place all ingredients in sprayed slow cooker and cook on LOW for 1 hour to 1 hour 30 minutes.

- Serve right from slow cooker. Stir before serving. Serves 6 to 8.

Bacon Dip with a Kick

1 (16 ounce) package cubed Mexican Velveeta® cheese	455 g
1 (10 ounce) can diced tomatoes and green chilies	280 g
1 tablespoon dry minced onion	15 ml
2 teaspoons Worcestershire sauce	10 ml
½ teaspoon dried mustard	2 ml
½ cup whipping cream or half-and-half cream	125 ml
16 slices bacon	

- Combine cubed cheese, tomatoes and green chilies, onion, Worcestershire, mustard, and cream in sprayed, small slow cooker.

- Turn heat to LOW, cover and cook for about 1 hour and stir several times to make sure cheese melts.

- While cheese is melting, place bacon in skillet, fry, drain and crumble.

- Fold three-fourths of bacon into cheese mixture.

- When ready to "dip", sprinkle remaining bacon on top and serve from slow cooker. Serves 4 to 6.

Dinner Dip

You can make a dinner out of this dip!

1 pound lean ground beef	455 g
1 small onion, very finely chopped	
2 (16 ounce) packages cubed Velveeta® cheese	2 (455 g)
2 (10 ounce) cans diced tomatoes and green chilies	2 (280 g)
1 teaspoon minced garlic	5 ml
Tortilla	

- Cook beef in skillet on low heat for 10 minutes, breaking up large chunks. Transfer to sprayed 4-quart (4 L) slow cooker.

- Add onion, cheese, tomatoes and green chilies, and garlic. Stir well.

- Cover and cook on LOW for 1 hour. Stir to mix well.

- Serve with tortilla chips. Serves 6 to 8.

Heavy-Duty Queso

1 pound bulk pork sausage	455 g
1 pound lean ground beef	455 g
1 cup hot salsa	265 g
1 (10 ounce) can cream of mushroom soup	280 g
1 (10 ounce) can diced tomatoes and green chilies	280 g
1 teaspoon garlic powder	5 ml
¾ teaspoon ground oregano	4 ml
2 (16 ounce) packages cubed Velveeta® cheese	2 (455 g)

- Cook sausage and ground beef in large skillet for 15 minutes and drain.

- Place in sprayed 4 to 5-quart (4 to 5 L) slow cooker.

- Add salsa, mushroom soup, tomatoes and green chilies, garlic powder, and oregano to saucepan and heat enough to mix well. Fold in cheese and pour into slow cooker.

- Cover and cook on LOW for 1 hour or until cheese melts. Stir once during cooking time.

- Serve from cooker. Serves 8 to 10.

Pizza Dunk

1 (6 ounce) package pepperoni	170 g
1 bunch green onions, thinly sliced	
½ red bell pepper, finely chopped	
1 medium tomato, finely chopped	
1 (14 ounce) jar pizza sauce	395 g
1½ cups shredded mozzarella cheese	175 g
1 (8 ounce) package cream cheese, cubed	230 g
Wheat crackers or tortilla chips	

- Chop pepperoni into small pieces and place in sprayed, small slow cooker. Add green onions, bell pepper, tomato and pizza sauce and stir well.

- Cover and cook on LOW for 2 hours 30 minutes to 3 hours 30 minutes. Stir in mozzarella and cream cheese and stir until they melt.

- Serve with wheat crackers or tortilla chips. Serves 4 to 6.

Corny Beef and Cheese

1 pound lean ground beef	455 g
1 onion, finely chopped	
1 (15 ounce) can whole kernel corn, drained	425 g
1 (16 ounce) jar salsa	455 g
1 (1 pound) package cubed Velveeta® cheese	455 g
Tortilla Chips	

- Brown and cook ground beef in skillet on low heat for about 10 minutes and drain. Transfer to sprayed slow cooker and add onion, corn, salsa and cheese.

- Cover and cook on LOW for 1 hour, remove lid and stir. Serve with tortilla chips. Serves 6 to 8.

Cheesy Border Bowl

2 pounds boneless, skinless chicken thighs, cubed	910 g
1 (10 ounce) can enchilada sauce	280 g
1 (7 ounce) can diced green chilies, drained	200 g
1 small onion, finely chopped	
1 large red bell pepper, finely chopped	
2 (8 ounce) packages cream cheese, cubed	2 (230 g)
1 (16 ounce) package shredded American cheese	455 g
Tortilla chips	

- Place chicken thighs, enchilada sauce, green chilies, onion and bell pepper in sprayed 4 to 5-quart (4 to 5 L) slow cooker.

- Cover and cook on LOW for 4 to 6 hours.

- Stir in cream cheese and American cheese and cook for additional 30 minutes. Stir several times during cooking. Serve with tortilla chips. Serves 8 to 10.

Golden Broccoli Dip

1 (16 ounce) box Mexican Velveeta® cheese, cubed	455 g
1 (10 ounce) can golden mushroom soup	280 g
¼ cup milk	60 ml
1 (10 ounce) box frozen chopped broccoli, thawed, drained	280 g

- Combine cheese, soup and milk in sprayed slow cooker, stir well and fold in broccoli.

- Cover and cook on LOW for 1 to 2 hours. Stir before serving. Serves 8 to 10.

Spicy Beef Dip

Men love this meaty, spicy dip.

2 pounds lean ground beef	910 g
2 tablespoons dried minced onion	30 ml
1½ teaspoons dried oregano leaves	7 ml
1 tablespoon chili powder	15 ml
2 teaspoons sugar	10 ml
1 (10 ounce) can diced tomatoes and green chilies	280 g
½ cup chili sauce	135 g
2 (16 ounce) packages cubed Mexican Velveeta® cheese	2 (455 g)
Chips or crackers	

- Brown ground beef in large skillet, drain and transfer to sprayed 4 to 5-quart (4 to 5 L) slow cooker.

- Add remaining ingredients plus ½ to 1 cup (125 to 250 ml) water and stir well.

- Cover and cook on LOW for 1 hour 30 minutes to 2 hours. Stir once or twice during cooking time.

- Add a little salt, if desired.

- Serve hot with chips or spread on crackers. Serves 8 to 10.

Big Bacon-Cheese Dip

2 (8 ounce) packages cream cheese, softened	**2 (230 g)**
1 (8 ounce) package shredded colby Jack cheese	**230 g**
2 tablespoons mustard	**30 ml**
2 teaspoons marinade for chicken	**30 ml**
4 green onions with tops, sliced	
1 - 2 pounds bacon, cooked, crumbled	**455 g**
Rye or pumpernickel bread	

- Cut cream cheese into cubes and place in sprayed 4 or 5-quart (4 to 5 L) slow cooker

- Add colby Jack cheese, mustard, marinade for chicken, green onions and ¼ teaspoon (1 ml) salt.

- Cover and cook on LOW for 1 hour and stir to melt cheese.

- Stir in crumbled bacon.

- Serve with small-size rye bread or toasted pumpernickel bread. Serves 6 to 8.

■ ■

■ *Keep the lid on the slow cooker (unless the recipe calls for stirring);* ■
■ *a slow cooker can take as long as 20 minutes to regain the heat lost* ■
■ *when the cover is removed. Do not cook without cover in place.* ■

■ ■

Dip-on-a-Chip

¾ cup (1½ sticks) butter	170 g
2 cups thinly sliced celery	200 g
1 onion, finely chopped	
3 tablespoons flour	20 g
1 (10 ounce) can cream of chicken soup	280 g
1 (10 ounce) box chopped broccoli, thawed	280 g
1 (5 ounce) garlic cheese roll, cut in chunks	145 g
Wheat crackers or corn chips	

- Melt butter in skillet and saute celery and onion, but do not brown; stir in flour.

- Spoon into sprayed, small slow cooker, stir in remaining ingredients and mix well.

- Cover and cook on LOW for 2 to 3 hours and stir several times.

- Serve with wheat crackers or corn chips. Serves 6 to 8.

After buying a new slow cooker, always read the manufacturer's information and directions. This will guide you in using the slow cooker properly as well as tell you about the various settings.

Jump-on-in Crab Dip

1 (8 ounce) package cream cheese, softened	230 g
1 (3 ounce) package cream cheese, softened	85 g
⅔ cup mayonnaise	150 g
1 tablespoon marinade for chicken	15 ml
1 tablespoon sherry or cooking sherry	15 ml
3 green onions with tops, chopped	
2 (6 ounce) cans crabmeat, drained, flaked	2 (170 g)

- Beat cream cheese, mayonnaise, 1 teaspoon (5 ml) salt and marinade for chicken in bowl and mix well with fork.

- Stir in sherry, green onions and crabmeat and spoon into sprayed, small slow cooker.

- Cover and cook on LOW for 1 hour 30 minutes to 2 hours and stir once. Serves 6 to 8.

Crab Dive

1 (6 ounce) can white crabmeat, drained, flaked	2 (170 g)
1 (8 ounce) package cream cheese, softened	230 g
½ cup (1 stick) butter, sliced	115 g
2 tablespoons white cooking wine	30 ml
Chips or crackers	

- Combine crabmeat, cream cheese, butter and wine in sprayed, small slow cooker.

- Cover and cook on LOW for 1 hour and gently stir to combine all ingredients.

- Serve from cooker with chips or crackers. Serves 4 to 6.

The word "Crock-Pot®" is a trademark of The Rival Company and refers to the crockery insert of its appliance with heating elements in the sides and bottom. It was introduced in 1971 and the cooking world changed.

Soups & Stews

Soups, Chilis, Stews, Chowders, Jambalayas

Soups & Stews Contents

Soups & Stews Contents

*If cooking soups or stews, leave at least 2 inches (5 cm)
of space between the top of the cooker and the food so that
the recipe can come to a simmer and not boil over.*

Mama's Minestrone

2 (15 ounce) cans Italian stewed tomatoes	2 (425 g)
2 (16 ounce) packages frozen vegetables and pasta in seasoned sauce	2 (455 g)
3 (14 ounce) cans beef broth	3 (395 g)
2 ribs celery, chopped	
2 potatoes, peeled, cubed	
1 teaspoon Italian herb seasoning	5 ml
2 (15 ounce) cans kidney beans, drained, rinsed	2 (425 g)
2 teaspoons minced garlic	10 ml

- Combine tomatoes, vegetables, broth, celery, potatoes, seasoning, beans, garlic and 1 cup (250 ml) water in sprayed, large slow cooker and mix well.

- Cover and cook on LOW for 4 to 6 hours. Serves 6 to 8.

Beans, Barley and Broth

2 (15 ounce) cans pinto beans with liquid	2 (425 g)
3 (14 ounce) cans chicken broth	3 (395 g)
½ cup quick-cooking barley	30 g
1 (15 ounce) can Italian stewed tomatoes	425 g

- Combine beans, broth, barley, stewed tomatoes and ½ teaspoon (2 ml) pepper in sprayed 6-quart (6 L) slow cooker and stir well.

- Cover and cook on LOW for 4 to 5 hours. Serves 6 to 8.

A Lotta Lentil Soup

2 (19 ounce) cans lentil home-style soup	2 (540 g)
1 (15 ounce) can stewed tomatoes	425 g
1 (14 ounce) can chicken broth	395 g
1 onion, chopped	
1 green bell pepper, chopped	
3 ribs celery, sliced	
1 carrot, halved, sliced	
2 teaspoons minced garlic	10 ml
1 teaspoon dried marjoram leaves	5 ml

- Combine all ingredients in sprayed slow cooker and stir well.

- Cover and cook on LOW for 5 to 6 hours. Serves 6 to 8.

Belle's Black Bean Soup

1 pound hot sausage	455 g
1 onion, chopped	
2 (14 ounce) cans chicken broth	2 (395 g)
2 (15 ounce) cans Mexican stewed tomatoes	2 (425 g)
1 green bell pepper, chopped	
2 (15 ounce) cans black beans, rinsed, drained	2 (425 g)

- Break up sausage and brown with onion in large skillet. Drain off fat and place sausage-onion mixture in sprayed, large slow cooker.

- Add chicken broth, stewed tomatoes, bell pepper, black beans and 1 cup (250 ml) water.

- Cover and cook on LOW for 3 to 5 hours. Serves 4 to 6.

Cream of Zucchini Soup

1 small onion, minced	
3½ - 4 cups grated zucchini with peel	440 - 500 g
2 (14 ounce) cans chicken broth	2 (395 g)
1 teaspoon seasoned salt	5 ml
1 teaspoon dried dill weed	5 ml
½ teaspoon white pepper	2 ml
2 tablespoons butter, melted	30 g
1 (8 ounce) carton sour cream	230 g

- Combine all ingredients except sour cream in sprayed, small slow cooker.

- Cover and cook on LOW for 2 hours.

- Fold in sour cream and continue cooking for about 10 minutes or just until soup is hot. Serves 4.

Long cooking time can cause dairy products to curdle. It is best to add ingredients such as sour cream, etc., near the end of cooking time.

7-Vegetable Soup

3 (14 ounce) cans chicken broth	3 (395 g)
¼ cup (½ stick) butter, melted	60 g
1 (16 ounce) package frozen mixed vegetables,	
thawed, drained	455 g
1 onion, chopped	
3 ribs celery, sliced	
1 teaspoon ground cumin	5 ml
3 zucchini, coarsely chopped	
2 cups chopped, fresh broccoli	180 g
1 cup half-and-half cream	250 ml

- Combine broth, butter, vegetables, onion, celery, cumin, and 1 teaspoon (5 ml) each of salt and pepper in sprayed, large slow cooker and stir well.

- Cover and cook on LOW for 6 to 7 hours or on HIGH for 3 to 4 hours.

- Stir in zucchini and broccoli. If not using HIGH temperature, turn heat to HIGH and cook for additional 30 minutes to 1 hour or until broccoli is tender-crisp.

- Turn off heat and stir in half-and-half cream. Let stand for 10 minutes before serving. Serves 6 to 8.

Cheesy Broccoli Soup

1 (16 ounce) package frozen chopped broccoli, thawed	455 g
1 (12 ounce) package cubed Velveeta® cheese	340 g
1 (2 ounce) packet white sauce mix	60 g
1 (1 ounce) packet vegetable soup mix	30 g
1 (12 ounce) can evaporated milk	355 ml
1 (14 ounce) can chicken broth	395 g

- Combine all ingredients plus 2 cups (500 ml) water in sprayed, large slow cooker and stir well.

- Cover and cook on LOW for 6 to 7 hours or on HIGH for 3 hours 30 minutes to 4 hours.

- Stir for 1 hour before serving time. Serves 4 to 6.

French Onion Soup

5 - 6 sweet onions, thinly sliced	
1 clove garlic, minced	
2 tablespoons butter	30 g
2 (14 ounce) cans beef broth	2 (425 g)
2 teaspoons Worcestershire sauce	10 ml
6 - 8 (1 inch/2.5 cm) slices French bread	
6 - 8 slices Swiss cheese	

- Cook onions and garlic in butter in large skillet on low heat (DO NOT BROWN) for about 20 minutes and stir several times.

- Transfer onion mixture to sprayed 4 to 5-quart (4 to 5 L) slow cooker. Add beef broth, Worcestershire and 1 cup (250 ml) water.

- Cover and cook on LOW for 5 to 8 hours or on HIGH for 2 hours 30 minutes to 4 hours.

- Before serving soup, toast bread slices with cheese slice on top. Broil for 3 to 4 minutes or until cheese is light brown and bubbly.

- Ladle soup into bowls and top with toast. Serves 6 to 8.

Northern Italian Soup

2 (15 ounce) cans great northern beans with liquid	**2 (425 g)**
2 (15 ounce) cans pinto beans with liquid	**2 (425 g)**
1 large onion, chopped	
1 tablespoon instant beef bouillon granules	**15 ml**
1 tablespoon minced garlic	**15 ml**
2 teaspoons Italian seasoning	**10 ml**
2 (15 ounce) cans Italian stewed tomatoes	**2 (425 g)**
1 (15 ounce) can cut green beans, drained	**425 g**

- Combine beans, onion, beef bouillon, garlic, Italian seasoning and 2 cups (500 ml) water in sprayed, large slow cooker.

- Cover and cook on LOW for 6 to 8 hours.

- Turn heat to HIGH, add stewed tomatoes and green beans and stir well.

- Continue cooking for additional 30 minutes or until green beans are tender. Serves 6 to 8.

TIP: Serve with crispy Italian toast.

Veggie Shells

2 yellow squash, peeled, chopped
2 zucchini, sliced
1 (10 ounce) package frozen whole kernel corn, thawed   280 g
1 red bell pepper, chopped
1 (15 ounce) can stewed tomatoes   425 g
1 teaspoon Italian seasoning   5 ml
2 teaspoons dried oregano   10 ml
2 (14 ounce) cans beef broth   2 (395 g)
¾ cup small shell pasta   55 g
Mozzarella cheese, optional

- Combine squash, zucchini, corn, bell pepper, tomatoes, seasonings, beef broth and 2 cups (500 ml) water in sprayed 6-quart (6 L) slow cooker.

- Cover and cook on LOW for 6 to 7 hours.

- Add pasta shells and cook and for additional 30 to 45 minutes or until pasta is tender.

- Garnish with a sprinkle of shredded mozzarella cheese on each bowl of soup, if desired. Serves 4 to 5.

Mean Bean Soup

4 (15 ounce) cans seasoned pinto beans with liquid	4 (425 g)
1 (10 ounce) package frozen seasoning blend (chopped onions and peppers)	280 g
2 cups chopped celery	200 g
2 (14 ounce) cans chicken broth	2 (395 g)
1 teaspoon Cajun seasoning	5 ml
⅛ teaspoon cayenne pepper	.5 ml

- Place all ingredients plus 1 cup (250 ml) water in sprayed 5-quart (5 L) slow cooker and stir well. Cover and cook on LOW 5 to 6 hours. Serves 6 to 8.

French Shells and Cheese

3 (10 ounce) cans tomato bisque soup	3 (280 g)
1 (10 ounce) can French onion soup	280 g
2 teaspoons Italian seasoning	10 ml
¾ cup tiny pasta shells	55 g
1½ cups shredded mozzarella cheese	175 g

- Place soups, Italian seasoning and 1½ soup cans water in sprayed 4 to 6-quart (4 to 6 L). Turn heat setting to HIGH and cook for 1 hour or until mixture is hot.

- Add pasta shells and cook for 1 hour 30 minutes to 2 hours or until pasta is cooked. Stir several times to keep pasta from sticking to bottom of slow cooker.

- Turn heat off, add mozzarella cheese and stir until cheese melts. Serves 6 to 8.

Cabbage with a Kick

1 pound lean ground beef	**455 g**
1 small head cabbage, chopped	
2 (15 ounce) cans jalapeno pinto beans with liquid	**2 (425 g)**
1 (15 ounce) can tomato sauce	**425 g**
1 (15 ounce) can Mexican stewed tomatoes	**425 g**
1 (14 ounce) can beef broth	**395 g**
2 teaspoons ground cumin	**10 ml**

- Brown ground beef in skillet, drain and place in sprayed 5 to 6-quart (5 to 6 L) slow cooker.

- Add cabbage, beans, tomato sauce, tomatoes, broth, cumin and 1 cup (250 ml) water and mix well.

- Cover and cook on LOW for 5 to 6 hours or until cabbage is tender. Serves 4 to 6.

Chicken Soup

2 (15 ounce) cans Mexican stewed tomatoes	2 (425 g)
2 (14 ounce) cans chicken broth	2 (395 g)
2 (10 ounce) cans chicken noodle soup	2 (280 g)
1 (15 ounce) can shoe-peg corn, drained	425 g
1 (15 ounce) can cut green beans, drained	425 g
1 (12 ounce) can diced chicken breast	340 g
Shredded pepper-Jack cheese	

- Place all ingredients except cheese in sprayed 4 to 5-quart (4 to 5 L) slow cooker and mix well.

- Cover and cook on LOW for 2 to 3 hours. Sprinkle shredded cheese over each bowl of soup. Serves 4 to 6.

Creamy Potato Soup

6 medium potatoes, peeled, cubed	
1 onion, minced	
2 (14 ounce) cans chicken broth	2 (395 g)
1 (8 ounce) package shredded American cheese	230 g
1 cup half-and-half cream	250 ml

- Combine potatoes, onion, chicken broth and ½ teaspoon (2 ml) pepper in sprayed slow cooker.

- Cover and cook on LOW for 8 to 10 hours. With potato masher, mash potatoes in slow cooker.

- About 1 hour before serving, stir in cheese and half-and-half cream and cook for 1 additional hour. Serves 4 to 6.

TIP: If you don't like black specks in your soup, use white pepper.

Hearty Beef Soup

1 pound lean ground beef	455 g
3 (14 ounce) cans beef broth	3 (395 g)
¾ cup quick-cooking barley	45 g
3 cups sliced carrots	385 g
2 cups sliced celery	200 g
2 teaspoons beef seasoning	10 ml

- Brown ground beef in skillet, drain and transfer to sprayed 5-quart (5 L) slow cooker. Add beef broth, barley, carrots, celery and beef seasoning.

- Cover and cook on LOW 7 to 8 hours. Serves 4.

Beefy Noodles

1½ pounds lean ground beef	680 g
1 onion, chopped	
2 (15 ounce) cans mixed vegetables, drained	2 (425 g)
2 (15 ounce) cans Italian stewed tomatoes	2 (425 g)
2 (14 ounce) cans beef broth	2 (395 g)
1 teaspoon dried oregano	5 ml
1 cup medium egg noodles	40 g

- Brown and cook ground beef in skillet until no longer pink and transfer to sprayed slow cooker.

- Add onion, mixed vegetables, stewed tomatoes, beef broth and oregano. Cover and cook on LOW for 4 to 5 hours.

- Cook noodles according to package direction. Add noodles to slow cooker and cook for additional 30 minutes. Serves 4 to 6.

3-B Soup

Beef and black beans – A yummy combination.

1 pound lean ground beef	**455 g**
2 onions, chopped	
2 cups sliced celery	**200 g**
2 (14 ounce) cans beef broth	**2 (395 g)**
1 (15 ounce) can Mexican stewed tomatoes	**425 g**
2 (15 ounce) cans black beans, rinsed, drained	**2 (425 g)**

- Brown beef in skillet until no longer pink. Place in sprayed 5 to 6-quart (5 to 6 L) slow cooker.

- Add onions, celery, broth, tomatoes, black beans, ¾ cup (175 ml) water, plus a little salt and pepper.

- Cover and cook on LOW for 6 to 7 hours or on HIGH for 3 hours to 3 hours 30 minutes. Serves 6 to 8.

TIP: If you like a zestier soup, add 1 teaspoon (5 ml) chili powder.

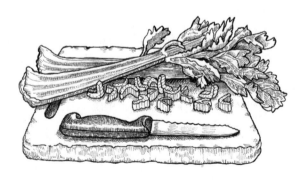

Supper Soup

1 pound lean beef stew meat	455 g
Seasoned pepper	
1 (14 ounce) can beef broth	395 g
1 (7 ounce) box beef-flavored rice and vermicelli mix	200 g
1 (10 ounce) package frozen peas and carrots	280 g
2½ cups vegetable juice	625 ml

- Sprinkle stew meat with seasoned pepper, brown in non-stick skillet, drain and place in sprayed, large slow cooker.

- Add broth, rice and vermicelli mix, peas and carrots, vegetable juice, and 2 cups (500 ml) water.

- Cover and cook on LOW for 6 to 7 hours. Serves 4 to 6.

Beef and Vegetable Twist

1 pound lean ground beef	455 g
1 (16 ounce) package coleslaw mix	455 g
1 (15 ounce) can cut green beans	425 g
1 (15 ounce) can whole kernel corn	425 g
2 (15 ounce) cans Italian stewed tomatoes	2 (425 g)
2 (14 ounce) cans beef broth	2 (395 g)
Cornbread	

- Brown ground beef in skillet, drain fat and place beef in sprayed, large slow cooker. Add slaw mix, green beans, corn, tomatoes and beef broth and sprinkle with a little salt and pepper.

- Cover and cook on LOW for 7 to 9 hours. Serve with cornbread. Serves 6 to 8.

It's Chilly Chili Soup

3 (15 ounce) cans chili with beans	3 (425 g)
1 (15 ounce) can whole kernel corn	425 g
1 (14 ounce) can beef broth	395 g
2 (15 ounce) cans Mexican stewed tomatoes	2 (425 g)
2 teaspoons ground cumin	10 ml
2 teaspoons chili powder	10 ml
Flour tortillas	

- Combine chili, corn, broth, tomatoes, cumin, chili powder and 1 cup (250 ml) water in sprayed 5 to 6-quart (5 to 6 L) slow cooker.

- Cover and cook on LOW for 4 to 5 hours. Serve with warm, buttered flour tortillas. Serves 6 to 8.

Veggie-Chili Soup

2 pounds lean ground beef	910 g
2 (15 ounce) cans chili without beans	2 (425 g)
1 (16 ounce) package frozen mixed vegetables, thawed	455 g
3 (14 ounce) cans beef broth	3 (395 g)
2 (15 ounce) cans stewed tomatoes	2 (425 g)
1 teaspoon seasoned salt	5 ml

- Brown ground beef in skillet until no longer pink. Place in sprayed 6-quart (6 L) slow cooker.

- Add chili, vegetables, broth, tomatoes, 1 cup (250 ml) water and seasoned salt and stir well.

- Cover and cook on LOW for 6 to 7 hours. Serves 6 to 8.

Whole Lotta Enchilada Soup

1 pound lean ground beef, browned, drained	455 g
1 (15 ounce) can Mexican stewed tomatoes	425 g
1 (15 ounce) can pinto beans with liquid	425 g
1 (15 ounce) can whole kernel corn with liquid	425 g
1 onion, chopped	
2 (10 ounce) cans enchilada sauce	2 (280 g)
1 (8 ounce) package shredded 4-cheese blend	230 g
Crushed tortilla chips, optional	

- Combine beef, tomatoes, beans, corn, onion, enchilada sauce and 1 cup (250 ml) water in sprayed 5 to 6-quart (5 to 6 L) slow cooker and mix well.

- Cover and cook on LOW for 6 to 8 hours or on HIGH for 3 to 4 hours.

- Stir in shredded cheese.

- If desired, top each serving with a few crushed tortilla chips. Serves 6 to 8.

Meatballs for All Soup

1 (32 ounce) package frozen meatballs	910 g
2 (15 ounce) cans stewed tomatoes	2 (425 g)
3 large potatoes, peeled, diced	
4 carrots, peeled, sliced	
2 medium onions, chopped	
2 (14 ounce) cans beef broth	2 (395 g)
2 tablespoons cornstarch	30 ml

- Combine meatballs, tomatoes, potatoes, carrots, onions, beef broth, a little salt and pepper, and 1 cup (250 ml) water in sprayed 6-quart (6 L) slow cooker.

- Cover and cook on LOW for 5 to 6 hours.

- Turn heat to HIGH and combine cornstarch with ¼ cup (60 ml) water in bowl. Pour into cooker and cook for additional 10 or 15 minutes or until slightly thick. Serves 4 to 6.

Tomato-Taco Soup

2 pounds lean ground beef	910 g
2 (15 ounce) cans ranch-style beans with liquid	2 (425 g)
1 (15 ounce) can whole kernel corn, drained	425 g
2 (15 ounce) cans stewed tomatoes	2 (425 g)
1 (10 ounce) can tomatoes and green chilies	280 g
1 (1 ounce) packet ranch dressing mix	30 g
1 (1 ounce) packet taco seasoning	30 g

- Brown ground beef in large skillet, drain and transfer to sprayed slow cooker.

- Add remaining ingredients and stir well.

- Cover and cook on LOW for 8 to 10 hours. Serves 6 to 8.

TIP: When serving, sprinkle shredded cheddar cheese over each serving.

Slow cookers meld flavors deliciously, but colors can fade over long cooking times, therefore you may want to dress up your dish with colorful garnishes such as fresh parsley or chives, salsa, extra shredded cheese, a sprinkle of paprika or a dollop of sour cream.

Tacos in a Bowl

1½ pounds lean ground beef	680 g
1 (1 ounce) packet taco seasoning	30 g
2 (15 ounce) cans Mexican stewed tomatoes	2 (425 g)
2 (15 ounce) cans chili beans with liquid	2 (425 g)
1 (15 ounce) can whole kernel corn, drained	425 g

Crushed tortilla chips
Shredded cheddar cheese

- Brown ground beef in skillet until it is no longer pink. Place in sprayed 5 to 6-quart (5 to 6 L) slow cooker. Add taco seasoning, tomatoes, chili beans, corn and 1 cup (250 ml) water and mix well.

- Cover and cook on LOW for 4 hours or on HIGH for 1 to 2 hours.

- Serve over crushed tortilla chips and sprinkle some shredded cheddar cheese over top of each serving. Serves 6 to 8.

Mexi-Ball Soup

3 (14 ounce) cans beef broth	3 (395 g)
1 (16 ounce) jar hot salsa	455 g
1 (16 ounce) package frozen whole kernel corn, thawed	455g
1 (16 ounce) package frozen meatballs, thawed	455g
1 teaspoon minced garlic	5 ml

- Combine all ingredients in sprayed slow cooker and stir well.

- Cover and cook on LOW for 5 to 7 hours. Serves 6 to 8.

Easy, Cheesy Potato Soup

5 medium potatoes, peeled, cubed	
2 cups cooked, cubed ham	280 g
1 cup fresh broccoli florets, cut very, very fine	90 g
1 (10 ounce) can cheddar cheese soup	280 g
1 (10 ounce) can fiesta nacho cheese soup	280 g
1 (14 ounce) can chicken broth	395 g
2½ soup cans milk	700 ml
Paprika	

- Place potatoes, ham and broccoli in sprayed slow cooker.

- Combine soups, broth and milk in saucepan. Heat just enough to mix until smooth. Stir into ingredients already in slow cooker.

- Cover and cook on LOW for 7 to 9 hours.

- When serving, sprinkle a little paprika over each serving. Serves 6 to 8.

- *For each 1 hour of cooking time in a conventional recipe, cook for 8 to 10 hours on LOW or 4 to 6 hours on HIGH in slow cooker.*

- *For each 45 minutes of cooking time in a conventional recipe, cook for 6 to 8 hours on LOW or 3 to 4 hours on HIGH in slow cooker.*

- *For each 30 minutes of cooking time in a conventional recipe, cook for 4 to 6 hours on LOW or 1 hour 30 minutes to 2 hours on HIGH.*

Double Sausage Soup

1 pound mild bulk sausage	455 g
1 pound hot bulk sausage	455 g
2 (15 ounce) cans Mexican stewed tomatoes	2 (425 g)
3 cups chopped celery	300 g
1 cup sliced carrots	130 g
1 (15 ounce) can cut green beans, drained	425 g
1 (14 ounce) can chicken broth	395 g
1 teaspoon seasoned salt	5 ml

- Combine mild and hot sausage in bowl, shape into small balls and place in non-stick skillet.

- Brown thoroughly and drain. Place in sprayed, large slow cooker.

- Add remaining ingredients plus 1 cup (250 ml) water and stir gently so meatballs will not break up.

- Cover and cook on LOW 6 to 7 hours. Serves 6 to 8.

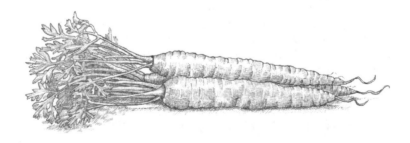

Down-South Soup

1½ cups dried black-eyed peas	225 g
2 - 3 cups cooked, cubed ham	280 - 420 g
1 (15 ounce) can whole kernel corn	425 g
1 (10 ounce) package frozen cut okra, thawed	280 g
1 onion, chopped	
1 large potato, cubed	
2 teaspoons Cajun seasoning	10 ml
1 (14 ounce) can chicken broth	395 g
2 (15 ounce) cans Mexican stewed tomatoes	2 (425 g)

- Rinse peas and drain. Combine peas and 5 cups (1.2 L) water in large saucepan.

- Bring to a boil, reduce heat, simmer for about 10 minutes and drain.

- Combine peas, ham, corn, okra, onion, potato, seasoning, broth and 2 cups (500 ml) water. in sprayed 5 to 6-quart (5 to 6 L) slow cooker

- Cover and cook on LOW for 6 to 8 hours.

- Add stewed tomatoes and continue cooking for additional 1 hour. Serves 6 to 8.

Ham-it-up Potato Soup

1 (1 ounce) packet white sauce mix	**30 g**
1 (28 ounce) package frozen hash-brown potatoes with onions and peppers	**795 g**
3 medium leeks, sliced	
3 cups cooked, cubed ham	**420 g**
1 (12 ounce) can evaporated milk	**375 ml**
1 (8 ounce) carton sour cream	**230 g**

- Pour 3 cups (750 ml) water in sprayed 4 to 5-quart (4 to 5 L) slow cooker and stir white sauce until smooth.

- Add hash-brown potatoes, leeks, ham and evaporated milk.

- Cover and cook on LOW for 7 to 9 hours or on HIGH for 3 hours 30 minutes to 4 hours 30 minutes.

- When ready to serve, turn heat to HIGH. Take out about 2 cups (500 ml) hot soup and pour into separate bowl. Stir in sour cream and return to cooker.

- Cover and continue cooking for 15 minutes or until mixture is thoroughly hot. Serves 6 to 8.

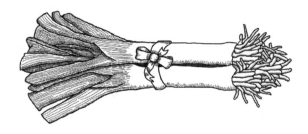

Vegetable-Pork Soup

2 pounds pork shoulder	910 g
1 onion, chopped	
2 ribs celery, sliced	
2 (15 ounce) cans yellow hominy with liquid	2 (425 g)
2 (15 ounce) cans stewed tomatoes	2 (425 g)
2 (14 ounce) cans chicken broth	2 (395 g)
1½ teaspoons ground cumin	7 ml
Tortillas	
Shredded cheese	
Chopped green onions	

- Cut pork into ½-inch (1.2 cm) cubes.

- Sprinkle pork cubes with a little salt and pepper and brown in skillet.

- Place in sprayed 5 to 6-quart (5 to 6 L) slow cooker.

- Combine onion, celery, hominy, stewed tomatoes, broth, cumin and 1 cup (250 ml) water in bowl.

- Pour over pork cubes.

- Cover and cook on HIGH for 6 to 7 hours.

- Serve with warm, buttered tortillas and top each bowl of soup with some shredded cheese and chopped green onions. Serves 6 to 8.

Navy Bean-Bacon Soup

8 slices thick-cut bacon, divided	
1 carrot	
3 (15 ounce) cans navy beans with liquid	3 (425 g)
3 ribs celery, chopped	
1 onion, chopped	
2 (14 ounce) cans chicken broth	2 (395 g)
1 teaspoon Italian seasoning	5 ml
1 (10 ounce) can cream of chicken soup	280 g

- Cook bacon in skillet, drain and crumble. (Reserve 2 crumbled slices for garnish.)

- Cut carrot in half lengthwise and slice.

- Combine most of crumbled bacon, carrot, beans, celery, onion, broth, seasoning and 1 cup (250 ml) water in sprayed 5 to 6-quart (5 to 6 L) slow cooker and stir to mix.

- Cover and cook on LOW for 5 to 6 hours.

- Ladle 2 cups (500 ml) soup mixture into food processor or blender and process until smooth.

- Return to cooker, add cream of chicken soup and stir well to mix.

- Turn heat to HIGH and cook for additional 10 to 15 minutes.
  Serves 6 to 8.

3-Pork Pasta Soup

1 onion, finely chopped	
2 ribs celery, chopped	
2 teaspoons minced garlic	**10 ml**
2 (14 ounce) cans chicken broth	**2 (395 g)**
2 (15 ounce) cans pork and beans with liquid	**2 (425 g)**
3 cups cooked, cubed ham	**420 g**
⅓ cup pasta shells	**25 g**
Bacon, cooked crisp, crumbled	

- Combine onion, celery, garlic, chicken broth, pork and beans, ham, and 1 cup (250 ml) water in sprayed 5 to 6-quart (5 to 6 L) slow cooker

- Cover and cook on LOW for 4 to 5 hours.

- Turn cooker to HIGH heat, add pasta and cook for additional 35 to 45 minutes or until pasta is tender.

- Garnish each serving with crumbled bacon. Serves 6 to 8.

Pizza Bowl

1 (16 ounce) package Italian link sausage, thinly sliced   455 g
1 onion, chopped
2 (4 ounce) cans sliced mushrooms   2 (115 g)
1 small green bell pepper, cored, seeded, julienned
1 (15 ounce) can Italian stewed tomatoes   425 g
1 (14 ounce) can beef broth   395 g
1 (8 ounce) can pizza sauce   230 g
Shredded mozzarella cheese

- Combine all ingredients except cheese in sprayed slow cooker and stir well.

- Cover and cook on LOW for 4 to 5 hours.

- Sprinkle mozzarella cheese over each serving. Serves 4 to 6.

Ham and Bean Soup

2 (14 ounce) cans chicken broth	2 (395 g)
3 (15 ounce) cans black beans, rinsed, drained	3 (425 g)
2 (10 ounce) cans diced tomatoes and green chilies	2 (280 g)
1 onion, chopped	
1 teaspoon ground cumin	5 ml
½ teaspoon dried thyme	2 ml
½ teaspoon dried oregano	2 ml
2 - 3 cups cooked, finely diced ham	280 - 420 g

- Combine chicken broth and black beans in sprayed slow cooker and turn cooker to HIGH.

- Cook just long enough for ingredients to get hot.

- With potato masher, mash about half of the beans in cooker.

- Reduce heat to LOW and add tomatoes and green chilies, onion, spices, diced ham and ¾ cup (175 ml) water.

- Cover and cook for 5 to 6 hours. Serves 6 to 8.

OOO-WEE! Bean Soup

1 (20 ounce) package Cajun-flavored, 16-bean soup mix
   with flavor packet   **570 g**
2 cups cooked, finely chopped ham   **280 g**
1 onion, chopped
2 (15 ounce) cans stewed tomatoes   **2 (425 g)**
Cornbread

- Soak beans overnight in large slow cooker. After soaking, drain water and cover with 2 inches (5 cm) water above beans.

- Cover and cook on LOW for 5 to 6 hours or until beans are tender.

- Add ham, onion, stewed tomatoes and flavor packet in bean soup mix.

- Cook on HIGH for 30 to 45 minutes.

- Serve with cornbread. Serves 4 to 6.

Black-Eyed Peas and Bacon Soup

5 slices thick-cut bacon, diced
1 onion, chopped
1 green bell pepper, chopped
3 ribs celery, sliced
3 (15 ounce) cans jalapeno black-eyed peas with liquid   3 (425 g)
2 (15 ounce) cans stewed tomatoes with liquid   2 (425 g)
1 teaspoon chicken seasoning   5 ml

- Cook bacon pieces until crisp in skillet, drain on paper towel and put in slow cooker.

- With bacon drippings in skillet, saute onion and bell peppers, but do not brown.

- To bacon in slow cooker, add onions, bell pepper, celery, black-eyed peas, stewed tomatoes, 1½ cups (375 ml) water, 1 teaspoon (5 ml) salt and chicken seasoning.

- Cover and cook on LOW for 3 to 4 hours. Serves 6 to 8.

Sausage Minestrone

1 pound Italian sausage links	455 g
2½ cups butternut or acorn squash	350 g
2 medium potatoes, peeled	
2 medium fennel bulbs, trimmed	
1 onion, chopped	
1 (15 ounce) can kidney beans, rinsed, drained	425 g
2 teaspoons minced garlic	10 ml
1 teaspoon Italian seasoning	5 ml
2 (14 ounce) cans chicken broth	2 (395 g)
1 cup dry white wine	250 ml
3 - 4 cups fresh spinach	90 - 120 g

- Cut sausage, potatoes and fennel into ½-inch (1.2 cm) slices.

- Cook sausage in skillet until brown and drain.

- Combine squash, potatoes, fennel, onion, beans, garlic and Italian seasoning in sprayed, large slow cooker.

- Top with sausage and pour chicken broth and wine over all.

- Cover and cook on LOW for 7 to 9 hours.

- Stir in spinach, cover and cook for additional 10 minutes.
  Serves 6 to 8.

Dark Bean and Sausage Soup

1 pound hot Italian sausage	**455 g**
1 onion, chopped	
1 (15 ounce) can Italian stewed tomatoes	**425 g**
2 (15 ounce) cans black beans, rinsed, drained	**2 (425 g)**
2 (15 ounce) cans navy beans with liquid	**2 (425 g)**
2 (14 ounce) cans beef broth	**2 (395 g)**
1 teaspoon minced garlic	**5 ml**
1 teaspoon dried basil	**5 ml**

- Cut sausage into ½-inch (1.2 cm) pieces.

- Brown sausage and onion in skillet, drain and transfer to sprayed 5 to 6-quart (5 to 6 L) slow cooker.

- Stir in tomatoes, black beans, navy beans, broth, garlic and basil and mix well.

- Cover and cook on LOW for 5 to 7 hours. Serves 6 to 8.

Chicken and Barley Soup

1½ - 2 pounds boneless, skinless chicken thighs	680 - 910 g
1 (16 ounce) package frozen stew vegetables	455 g
1 (1 ounce) packet dry vegetable soup mix	30 g
1¼ cups pearl barley	250 g
2 (14 ounce) cans chicken broth	2 (395 g)
1 teaspoon white pepper	5 ml

- Combine all ingredients with 1 teaspoon (5 ml) salt and 4 cups (1 L) water in sprayed, large slow cooker.

- Cover and cook on LOW for 5 to 6 hours or on HIGH for 3 hours. Serves 6 to 8.

Cheddar-Chicken Soup

2 cups milk	500 ml
1 (7 ounce) package cheddar-broccoli soup starter	200 g
1 cup cooked, finely chopped chicken breasts	140 g
1 (10 ounce) frozen green peas, thawed	280 g
Shredded cheddar cheese	

- Place 5 cups (1.2 L) water and 2 cups milk in sprayed slow cooker. Set heat on HIGH until water and milk come to a boil. Stir contents of soup starter into slow cooker and stir well. Add chopped chicken, green peas and a little salt and pepper.

- Cook on LOW for 2 to 3 hours.

- To serve, sprinkle cheddar cheese over each serving of soup. Serves 4.

So Simple Chicken and Rice

1 (6 ounce) package long grain-wild rice mix	170 g
1 (1 ounce) packet chicken noodle soup mix	30 g
2 (10 ounce) cans cream of chicken soup	2 (280 g)
2 ribs celery, chopped	
1 - 2 cups cooked, cubed chicken	140 - 280 g

- Combine all ingredients and about 6 cups (1.4 L) water in sprayed 5 to 6-quart (5 to 6 L) slow cooker.

- Cover and cook on LOW for 2 to 3 hours. Serves 4 to 6.

A Little Italy Soup

1½ pounds boneless, skinless chicken thighs, cubed	680 g
1 onion, chopped	
3 carrots, sliced	
½ cup halved, pitted ripe olives	65 g
1 teaspoon minced garlic	5 ml
3 (14 ounce) cans chicken broth	3 (395 g)
1 (15 ounce) can Italian stewed tomatoes	425 g
1 teaspoon Italian seasoning	5 ml
½ cup small shell pasta	40 g
Parmesan cheese	

- Combine all ingredients except shell pasta and parmesan cheese in sprayed slow cooker.

- Cover and cook on LOW for 8 to 9 hours. About 30 minutes before serving, add pasta and stir.

- Increase heat to HIGH and cook for additional 20 to 30 minutes. Garnish with parmesan cheese. Serves 6 to 8.

Colorful Chicken Soup

1 pound skinless, boneless chicken thighs	455 g
1 (6.2 ounce) package chicken and herb-flavored rice	170 g
3 (14 ounce) cans chicken broth	3 (395 g)
3 carrots, sliced	
1 (10 ounce) can cream of chicken soup	280 g
1½ tablespoons chicken seasoning	22 ml
1 (10 ounce) package frozen whole kernel corn, thawed	280 g
1 (10 ounce) package frozen baby green peas, thawed	280 g

- Cut thighs in thin strips.

- Combine chicken, rice, chicken broth, carrots, soup, seasoning and 1 cup (250 ml) water in sprayed 5 to 6-quart (5 to 6 L) slow cooker.

- Cover and cook on LOW for 8 to 9 hours.

- About 30 minutes before serving, turn heat to HIGH and add corn and peas to cooker. Continue cooking for additional 30 minutes. Serves 4 to 6.

Slow cookers work best when filled to between two-thirds and three-quarters of capacity.

Spinach-Cheese Tortellini

1 (1 ounce) packet white sauce mix	30 g
3 boneless, skinless chicken breast halves	
1 (14 ounce) can chicken broth	395 g
1 teaspoon minced garlic	5 ml
½ teaspoon dried basil	2 ml
½ teaspoon oregano	2 ml
½ teaspoon cayenne pepper	2 ml
1 (8 ounce) package cheese tortellini	230 g
1½ cups half-and-half cream	375 ml
6 cups fresh baby spinach	180 g

- Place white sauce mix in sprayed 5 to 6-quart (5 to 6 L) slow cooker.

- Stir in 4 cups (1 L) water and stir gradually until mixture is smooth.

- Cut chicken into 1-inch (2.5 cm) pieces. Add chicken, broth, garlic, basil, oregano, cayenne pepper and ½ teaspoon (2 ml) salt to mixture.

- Cover and cook on LOW for 6 to 7 hours or on HIGH for 3 hours.

- Stir in tortellini, cover and cook for additional 1 hour on HIGH.

- Stir in half-and-half cream and fresh spinach and cook just enough for soup to get hot. Serves 4 to 6.

TIP: Sprinkle a little shredded parmesan cheese on top of each serving.

Tortilla Soup

3 large boneless, skinless chicken breast halves, cubed
1 (10 ounce) package frozen whole kernel corn, thawed   **280 g**
1 onion, chopped
3 (14 ounce) cans chicken broth   **3 (395 g)**
1 (6 ounce) can tomato paste   **170 g**
2 (10 ounce) cans diced tomatoes and green chilies   **2 (280 g)**
2 teaspoons ground cumin   **10 ml**
1 teaspoon chili powder   **5 ml**
1 teaspoon minced garlic   **5 ml**
6 corn tortillas

- Combine chicken cubes, corn, onion, broth, tomato paste, tomatoes and green chilies, cumin, chili powder, 1 teaspoon (5 ml) salt, and garlic in sprayed, large slow cooker.

- Cover and cook on LOW for 5 to 7 hours or on HIGH for 3 hours to 3 hours 30 minutes.

- While soup is cooking, cut tortillas into ¼-inch (6 mm) strips and place on baking sheet.

- Bake at 375° (190° C) for about 5 minutes or until crisp.

- Serve baked tortilla strips with soup. Serves 6 to 8.

Not Just Chicken and Rice

1 pound boneless, skinless chicken breasts	455 g
½ cup brown rice	95 g
1 (10 ounce) can cream of chicken soup	280 g
1 (10 ounce) can cream of celery soup	280 g
1 (14 ounce) can chicken broth with roasted garlic	395 g
1 (16 ounce) package frozen sliced carrots, thawed	455 g
1 cup half-and-half cream	250 ml

- Cut chicken into 1-inch pieces. Place pieces in sprayed 4 to 5-quart (4 to 5 L) slow cooker.

- Combine rice, soups, chicken broth and carrots in saucepan, heat just enough to mix well and pour over chicken.

- Cover and cook on LOW for 7 to 8 hours.

- Turn heat to HIGH, add half-and-half cream and cook for additional 15 to 20 minutes. Serves 6 to 8.

Mexican Turkey Soup

This is great for leftover turkey.

2 (14 ounce) cans chicken broth	2 (395 g)
2 (15 ounce) cans Mexican stewed tomatoes	2 (425 g)
1 (16 ounce) package frozen succotash, thawed	455 g
2 teaspoons chili powder	10 ml
1 teaspoon dried cilantro	5 ml
2 cups crushed tortilla chips, divided	175 g
2½ cups cooked, chopped turkey	350 g

- Combine broth, tomatoes, succotash, chili powder, cilantro, ⅓ cup (30 g) crushed tortilla chips and turkey in sprayed, large slow cooker and stir well.

- Cover and cook on LOW for 3 to 5 hours. When ready to serve, sprinkle remaining chips over each serving. Serves 6 to 8.

TIP: Do not use smoked turkey.

Shitake-Turkey Soup

Another great way to use leftover chicken or turkey

2 cups sliced shitake mushrooms	**145 g**
2 ribs celery, sliced	
1 small onion, chopped	
2 tablespoons butter	**30 g**
1 (15 ounce) can sliced carrots	**425 g**
2 (14 ounce) cans chicken broth	**2 (395 g)**
½ cup orzo pasta	**85 g**
2 cups cooked, chopped turkey	**280 g**

- Saute mushrooms, celery and onion in butter in skillet.

- Transfer vegetables to slow cooker and add carrots, broth, orzo and turkey.

- Cover and cook on LOW for 2 to 3 hours or on HIGH for 1 to 2 hours. Serves 4 to 6.

TIP: Do not use smoked turkey in this recipe.

Taco Stew

2 pounds very lean stew meat	**910 g**
2 (15 ounce) cans Mexican stewed tomatoes	**2 (425 g)**
1 (1 ounce) packet taco seasoning mix	**30 g**
2 (15 ounce) cans pinto beans with liquid	**2 (425 g)**
1 (15 ounce) can whole kernel corn with liquid	**425 g**

- Cut large pieces of stew meat in half and brown in large skillet.

- Combine stew meat, tomatoes, taco seasoning mix, beans, corn and ¾ cup (175 ml) water in sprayed 4 to 5-quart (4 to 5 L) slow cooker. (If you are not into "spicy", use original recipe stewed tomatoes instead of Mexican.)

- Cover and cook on LOW for 5 to 7 hours. Serves 6 to 8.

TIP: For garnish, top each serving with chopped green onions.

Not only does a slow cooker give out less heat to make the house hot, it uses less electricity than an electric oven.

4-Corner Stew

A hearty, filling soup.

1½ pounds lean ground beef	680 g
1 (14 ounce) can beef broth	395 g
1 (15 ounce) can whole kernel corn with liquid	425 g
2 (15 ounce) cans pinto beans with liquid	2 (425 g)
2 (15 ounce) cans Mexican stewed tomatoes	2 (425 g)
1 tablespoon beef seasoning	15 ml
1 (16 ounce) package cubed Velveeta® cheese	455 g

- Brown beef in skillet until no longer pink.

- Place in sprayed 5 to 6-quart (5 to 6 L) slow cooker and add broth, corn, beans, tomatoes and beef seasoning.

- Cook on LOW for 5 to 6 hours.

- When ready to serve, fold in cheese and stir until cheese melts. Serves 6 to 8.

TIP: Cornbread is a must to serve with this stew.

Real Roast Beef Stew

3 cups cubed roast beef	420 g
2 (15 ounce) cans stewed tomatoes	2 (425 g)
1 (16 ounce) package frozen mixed vegetables, thawed	455 g
2 (14 ounce) cans beef broth	2 (395 g)
1 cup cauliflower florets	100 g
1 cup broccoli florets	70 g

- Combine all ingredients except cauliflower and broccoli in sprayed 6-quart (6 L) slow cooker. Add a little salt and pepper.

- Cover and cook on LOW for 3 to 4 hours.

- Stir in cauliflower and broccoli and continue cooking for additional 2 hours until tender. Serves 6 to 8.

South-of-the-Border Stew

1½ - 2 pounds lean beef stew meat	680 - 910 g
2 (15 ounce) cans pinto beans with liquid	2 (425 g)
1 onion, chopped	
3 carrots, sliced	
2 medium potatoes, cubed	
1 (1 ounce) packet taco seasoning	30 g
2 (15 ounce) cans Mexican stewed tomatoes	2 (425 g)

- Brown stew meat in non-stick skillet. Combine meat, pinto beans, onion, carrots, potatoes, taco seasoning and 2 cups (500 ml) water in sprayed, large slow cooker.

- Cover and cook on LOW for 6 to 7 hours. Add stewed tomatoes and cook for additional 1 hour. Serves 4 to 6.

TIP: This is great served with warmed, buttered, flour tortillas.

Meatball Stew

1 (18 ounce) package frozen Italian meatballs, thawed	510 g
1 (14 ounce) can beef broth	395 g
1 (15 ounce) can cut green beans	425 g
1 (16 ounce) package baby carrots	455 g
2 (15 ounce) cans stewed tomatoes	2 (425 g)
1 tablespoon Worcestershire sauce	15 ml
½ teaspoon ground allspice	2 ml

- Combine all ingredients in sprayed slow cooker.

- Cover and cook on LOW for 3 to 5 hours. Serves 4 to 6.

Mixed Veggie and Meatball Stew

1 (18 ounce) package frozen cooked meatballs, thawed	510 g
1 (16 ounce) package frozen mixed vegetables, thawed	455 g
1 (15 ounce) can stewed tomatoes	425 g
1 (12 ounce) jar beef gravy	340 g
2 teaspoons crushed dried basil	10 ml

- Place meatballs and mixed vegetables in sprayed 4 to 5-quart (4 to 5 L) slow cooker.

- Combine stewed tomatoes, gravy, basil, ½ teaspoon (2 ml) pepper and ½ cup (125 ml) water in bowl. Pour over meatballs and vegetables.

- Cover and cook on LOW for 6 to 7 hours. Serves 4 to 6.

Meat and Potatoes Stew

1 (28 ounce) package frozen meatballs, thawed	795 g
2 (15 ounce) cans Italian stewed tomatoes	2 (425 g)
2 (14 ounce) cans beef broth	2 (395 g)
2 (15 ounce) cans new potatoes	2 (425 g)
1 (16 ounce) package baby carrots	455 g
1 tablespoon beef seasoning	15 ml

- Place meatballs, stewed tomatoes, beef broth, potatoes, carrots and beef seasoning in sprayed 6-quart (6 L) slow cooker.

- Cover and cook on LOW for 6 to 7 hours.

- Serve with corn muffins. Serves 6 to 8.

Southern Salsa Stew

1½ - 2 pounds boneless, beef chuck roast	680 - 910 g
1 green bell pepper	
2 onions, coarsely chopped	
2 (15 ounce) cans pinto beans with liquid	2 (425 g)
½ cup rice	95 g
1 (14 ounce) can beef broth	395 g
2 (15 ounce) cans Mexican stewed tomatoes	2 (425 g)
1 cup mild or medium green salsa	265 g
2 teaspoons ground cumin	10 ml
Flour tortillas	

- Trim fat from beef and cut into 1-inch (2.5 cm) cubes. Brown beef in large skillet and place in large, sprayed slow cooker.

- Cut bell pepper into ½-inch (1.2 cm) slices. Add remaining ingredients except tortillas, 1½ cups (375 ml) water and a little salt.

- Cover and cook on LOW for 7 to 8 hours.

- Serve with warm flour tortillas. Serves 6 to 8.

Sweet-n-Sour Stew

2 pounds premium lean beef stew meat	910 g
1 (16 ounce) package frozen Oriental stir-fry vegetables, thawed	455 g
1 (10 ounce) can beefy mushroom soup	280 g
1 (10 ounce) can beef broth	280 g
⅔ cup sweet-and-sour sauce	150 ml
1 tablespoon beef seasoning	15 ml

- Sprinkle stew meat with ½ teaspoon (5 ml) pepper in skillet and brown. Place in sprayed slow cooker.

- Combine vegetables, soup, broth, sweet-and-sour sauce, beef seasoning and 1 cup (250 ml) water in bowl. Pour over stew meat and stir well.

- Cover and cook on LOW for 5 to 7 hours. Serves 4 to 6.

Chicken-Cheese Tortellini

1 (9 ounce) package cheese-filled tortellini	255 g
2 medium yellow squash, halved, sliced	
1 red bell pepper, coarsely chopped	
1 onion, chopped	
2 (14 ounce) cans chicken broth	2 (395 g)
1 teaspoon dried rosemary	5 ml
½ teaspoon dried basil	2 ml
2 cups cooked, chopped chicken	280 g

- Place tortellini, squash, bell pepper and onion in sprayed slow cooker. Stir in broth, rosemary, basil and chicken.

- Cover and cook on LOW for 2 to 4 hours or until tortellini and vegetables are tender. Serves 4.

Chicken Italy

4 large boneless, skinless chicken breast halves, cubed	
3 medium potatoes, peeled, cubed	
1 (26 ounce) jar meatless spaghetti sauce	740 g
1 (15 ounce) can cut green beans, drained	425 g
1 (15 ounce) can whole kernel corn	425 g
1 tablespoon chicken seasoning	15 ml

- Combine all ingredients and ¾ cup (175 ml) water in sprayed 5 to 6-quart (5 to 6 L) slow cooker.

- Cover and cook on LOW for 6 to 7 hours. Serves 4 to 6.

Chicken on a Biscuit

2 (1 ounce) packets chicken gravy mix	**2 (30 g)**
2 cups sliced celery	**200 g**
1 (10 ounce) package frozen sliced carrots	**280 g**
1 (10 ounce) package frozen green peas, thawed	**280 g**
1 teaspoon dried basil	**5 ml**
3 cups cooked, cubed chicken	**420 g**
Buttermilk biscuits	

- Combine gravy mix, 2 cups (500 ml) water, celery, carrots, peas, basil, ¾ teaspoon (4 ml) each of salt and pepper, and chicken in sprayed slow cooker.

- Cover and cook on LOW for 6 to 7 hours. Serve over baked buttermilk biscuits. Serves 4 to 6.

TIP: If you like thick stew, mix 2 tablespoons (15 g) cornstarch with ¼ cup (60 ml) water and stir into chicken mixture. Cook for additional 30 minutes to thicken.

Trail Ride Stew

3 cups cooked, diced ham	420 g
1 pound smoked sausage	455 g
3 (14 ounce) cans chicken broth	3 (395 g)
1 (15 ounce) can diced tomatoes	425 g
1 (7 ounce) can diced green chilies	200 g
1 onion, chopped	
2 (15 ounce) cans pinto beans with liquid	2 (425 g)
1 (15 ounce) can whole kernel corn	425 g
1 teaspoon garlic powder	5 ml
2 teaspoons ground cumin	10 ml
2 teaspoons cocoa	10 ml
1 teaspoon dried oregano	5 ml

- Cut sausage into ½-inch (1.2 cm) pieces.

- Combine all ingredients and 1 teaspoon (5 ml) salt in sprayed slow cooker and stir well.

- Cover and cook on LOW for 5 to 7 hours.

- Serve with buttered, flour tortillas. Serves 6 to 8.

Southern Sunday Stew

This ham and vegetable stew is great served with cornbread.

2 cups dried black-eyed peas	300 g
3 cups cooked, cubed ham	420 g
1 large onion, chopped	
2 cups sliced celery	200 g
1 (15 ounce) can yellow hominy, drained	425 g
2 (15 ounce) cans stewed tomatoes	2 (425 g)
1 (14 ounce) can chicken broth	395 g
2 teaspoons seasoned salt	10 ml
2 tablespoons cornstarch	30 ml

- Rinse and drain dried black-eyed peas in saucepan. Cover peas with water, bring to a boil and drain again.

- Place peas in sprayed, large slow cooker and add 5 cups (1.2 L) water, ham, onion, celery, hominy, tomatoes, broth and seasoned salt.

- Cover and cook on LOW for 7 to 9 hours.

- Mix cornstarch with ⅓ cup (75 ml) water in bowl, turn cooker to HIGH heat, pour in cornstarch mixture and stir well.

- Cook for about 10 minutes or until stew thickens. Add good amount of salt and pepper and stir well before serving. Serves 6 to 8.

TIP: If you would like a little spice in the stew, substitute a can of Mexican stewed tomatoes for one of the cans of stewed tomatoes.

Spicy Sausage Stew

1 (16 ounce) package smoked sausage links	455 g
1 (28 ounce) can baked beans with liquid	795 g
1 (15 ounce) can great northern beans with liquid	425 g
1 (15 ounce) can pinto beans with liquid	425 g
1 (15 ounce) can lentil soup	425 g
1 onion, chopped	
1 teaspoon Cajun seasoning	5 ml
2 (15 ounce) cans stewed tomatoes	2 (425 g)
Corn muffins	

- Peel skin from sausage links and slice. Place in sprayed 6-quart (6 L) slow cooker, add remaining ingredients and stir to mix.

- Cover and cook on LOW for 3 to 4 hours.

- Serve with corn muffins. Serves 6 to 8.

You can thicken liquid in the slow cooker by mixing 1 tablespoon (15 ml) cornstarch with 2 tablespoons (30 ml) cold water. Add to liquid and cook until liquid reaches gravy/sauce consistency.

Vegetable and Tenderloin Stew

1 (2 pound) pork tenderloin	**910 g**
1 onion, coarsely chopped	
1 red bell pepper, seeded, julienned	
1 (16 ounce) package frozen mixed vegetables, thawed	**455 g**
2 tablespoons flour	**15 g**
½ teaspoon dried rosemary leaves	**2 ml**
½ teaspoon oregano leaves	**2 ml**
1 (14 ounce) can chicken broth	**395 g**
1 (6 ounce) package long grain-wild rice	**170 g**

- Cut tenderloin into 1-inch (2.5 cm) cubes.

- Brown tenderloin in non-stick skillet and place in large, sprayed slow cooker.

- Add onion, bell pepper and mixed vegetables.

- Combine flour, rosemary and oregano with chicken broth in bowl and pour over vegetables.

- Cover and cook on LOW for 4 to 4 hours 30 minutes.

- When ready to serve, cook rice according to package directions.

- Serve pork and vegetables over rice. Serves 4 to 6.

Italian-Sausage Stew

1½ - 2 pounds Italian sausage	680 - 910 g
2 (16 ounce) packages frozen vegetables	2 (455 g)
2 (15 ounce) cans Italian stewed tomatoes	2 (425 g)
1 (14 ounce) can beef broth	395 g
1 teaspoon Italian seasoning	5 ml
½ cup pasta shells	40 g

- Brown and cook sausage in skillet for about 5 minutes and drain.

- Combine sausage, vegetables, stewed tomatoes, broth, Italian seasoning and shells in sprayed 5 to 6-quart (5 to 6 L) slow cooker and mix well.

- Cover and cook on LOW for 3 to 5 hours. Serves 4 to 6.

Hungry Hungarian Stew

2 pounds boneless short ribs	910 g
1 cup pearl barley	200 g
1 small onion, chopped	
1 green bell pepper, cored, seeded, chopped	
1 teaspoon minced garlic	5 ml
2 (15 ounce) cans kidney beans, drained	2 (425 g)
2 (14 ounce) cans beef broth	2 (395 g)
1 tablespoon paprika	15 ml

- Combine all ingredients plus 1 cup (250 ml) water in sprayed slow cooker.

- Cover and cook on LOW for 8 to 9 hours or on HIGH for 4 hours 30 minutes to 5 hours. Serves 4 to 6.

Ham-Cabbage Stew

2 (15 ounce) can Italian stewed tomatoes	**2 (425 g)**
3 cups shredded cabbage	**210 g**
1 onion, chopped	
1 red bell pepper, cored, seeded, chopped	
2 tablespoons butter, sliced	**30 g**
1 (14 ounce) can chicken broth	**395 g**
¾ teaspoon seasoned salt	**4 ml**
3 cups cooked, diced ham	**420 g**

- Combine all ingredients and ¾ teaspoons (4 ml) pepper with 1 cup (250 ml) water in sprayed, large slow cooker and stir to mix well.

- Cover and cook on LOW for 5 to 7 hours. Serve with cornbread. Serves 4 to 6.

Creamy Veggie Stew

1½ pounds select stew meat	680 g
2 (10 ounce) cans French onion soup	2 (280 g)
1 (10 ounce) can cream of onion soup	280 g
1 (10 ounce) can cream of celery soup	280 g
1 (16 ounce) package frozen stew vegetables, thawed	455 g

- Place stew meat in sprayed slow cooker. Add soups and vegetables and spread each evenly over meat in layers. DO NOT STIR.

- Turn slow cooker to HIGH and cook just long enough for ingredients to get hot. Change heat setting to LOW, cover and cook for 7 to 8 hours. Serves 4 to 6.

Meatless Chili

2 (15 ounce) cans stewed tomatoes	2 (425 g)
1 (15 ounce) can kidney beans, rinsed, drained	425 g
1 (15 ounce) can pinto beans with liquid	425 g
1 onion, chopped	
1 green bell pepper, seeded, chopped	
1 tablespoon chili powder	15 ml
1 (7 ounce) package elbow macaroni	200 g
¼ cup (½ stick) butter, sliced	60 g
Shredded cheddar cheese	

- Combine tomatoes, kidney beans, pinto beans, onion, bell pepper, chili powder and 1 cup (250 ml) water in sprayed 4 to 5-quart (4 to 5 L) slow cooker.

- Cover and cook on LOW for 4 to 5 hours or on HIGH for 2 hours.

- Cook macaroni according to package directions, drain and stir butter into hot macaroni. Fold into chili.

- If desired, top each serving with shredded cheddar cheese. Serves 4 to 6.

Chicken Chili

3 (15 ounce) cans navy beans with liquid	3 (425 g)
3 (14 ounce) cans chicken broth	3 (395 g)
1 (10 ounce) can cream of chicken soup	280 g
2 tablespoons butter, melted	30 g
2 onions, chopped	
3 cups cooked, chopped chicken or turkey	420 g
1 (7 ounce) can diced green chilies	200 g
1 teaspoon minced garlic	5 ml
½ teaspoon dried basil	2 ml
½ teaspoon white pepper	2 ml
⅛ teaspoon cayenne pepper	.5 ml
⅛ teaspoon ground cloves	.5 ml
1 teaspoon ground oregano	5 ml
1 (8 ounce) package shredded 4-cheese blend	230 g

• Combine all ingredients except cheese in sprayed slow cooker.

• Cover and cook on LOW for 4 to 5 hours.

• When serving, sprinkle cheese over top of each serving. Serves 6 to 8.

Veggie Chili

2 (15 ounce) cans navy beans with liquid	**2 (425 g)**
1 (15 ounce) can pinto beans with liquid	**425 g**
2 (15 ounce) cans Mexican stewed tomatoes	**2 (425 g)**
1 (15 ounce) can whole kernel corn	**425 g**
1 onion, chopped	
3 ribs celery, sliced	
1 tablespoon chili powder	**15 ml**
2 teaspoons dried oregano leaves	**10 ml**
1 teaspoon seasoned salt	**5 ml**
Broccoli cornbread	

- Combine beans, tomatoes, corn, onion, celery, chili powder, oregano, seasoned salt and 1½ cups (375 ml) water in sprayed 5 to 6-quart (5 to 6 L) slow cooker.

- Cover and cook on LOW for 4 to 6 hours.

- Serve with hot, buttered broccoli cornbread. Serves 6 to 8.

You may want to invest in two slow cookers so both a main dish and a side dish or dessert can cook at the same time. Select two different sizes for greater versatility. If you like hot dips, a mini slow cooker is ideal.

Homemade Chili

2 pounds lean beef chili meat	**910 g**
1 large onion, finely chopped	
1 (10 ounce) can diced tomatoes and green chilies	**280 g**
2½ cups tomato juice	**625 ml**
2 tablespoons chili powder	**30 ml**
1 tablespoon ground cumin	**15 ml**
1 tablespoon minced garlic	**15 ml**
1 (15 ounce) can pinto or kidney beans	**425 g**

- Combine chili meat, onion, tomatoes and green chilies, tomato juice, chili powder, cumin, garlic, and 1 cup (250 ml) water in sprayed, large slow cooker and mix well.

- Cover and cook on LOW for 7 to 9 hours.

- Add pinto or kidney beans and continue to cook for additional 30 minutes. Serves 4 to 6.

Last-Minute Chili

4 pounds lean ground beef	1.8 kg
2 (10 ounce) packages hot chili mix	2 (280 g)
1 (6 ounce) can tomato sauce	170 g
2 (15 ounce) cans stewed tomatoes with liquid	2 (425 g)
2½ teaspoons ground cumin	12 ml

- Break ground beef into pieces and brown in large skillet and drain. Use slotted spoon to drain fat and place beef in sprayed 5 to 6-quart (5 to 6 L) slow cooker.

- Add chili mix, tomato sauce, stewed tomatoes, cumin, 1 teaspoon (5 ml) salt and 1 cup (250 ml) water.

- Cover and cook on LOW setting for 4 to 5 hours. If you think you can't eat chili without beans, add 2 (15 ounce/425 g) cans Ranch Style® or chili beans. Serves 6 to 8.

Beefy Chili

2 pounds premium cut stew meat	910 g
1 onion, chopped	
2 (15 ounce) cans diced tomatoes	2 (425 g)
2 (15 ounce) cans pinto beans with liquid	2 (425 g)
1½ tablespoons chili powder	22 ml
2 teaspoons ground cumin	10 ml
1 teaspoon ground oregano	5 ml
Shredded cheese	

- If stew meat is in fairly large chunks, cut each chunk in half.

- Brown stew meat in large skillet and transfer to sprayed, large slow cooker.

- Add onion, tomatoes, beans, seasonings and a little salt.

- Cover and cook on LOW for 6 to 7 hours.

- Sprinkle shredded cheddar cheese over each serving. Serves 4 to 6.

Ham Chowder

1 medium potato
3 cups cooked, cubed ham   420 g
1 (16 ounce) bag split peas, rinsed   455 g
1 (11 ounce) can whole kernel corn with red and green peppers 310 g
1 (14 ounce) can chicken broth   395 g
2 carrots, sliced
2 ribs celery, diagonally sliced
1 tablespoon dried onion flakes   15 ml
1 teaspoon dried marjoram leaves   5 ml
1 teaspoon seasoned salt   5 ml

- Cut potato into small cubes and add to sprayed slow cooker.

- Add remaining ingredients plus 3 cups (750 ml) water and 1 teaspoon (5 ml) salt.

- Cover and cook on LOW for 6 to 8 hours. Serves 4 to 6.

Purchase a slow cooker that has a removable ceramic bowl; it is easier to clean and there won't be a chance of getting the power cord wet. Allow cooker to cool completely before washing or soaking. With most models, the removable bowl can be used as the serving dish.

Corny Ham Chowder

A great recipe for leftover ham.

1 medium potato	
2 (10 ounce) cans cream of celery soup	2 (280 g)
1 (14 ounce) can chicken broth	395 g
3 cups finely diced ham	420 g
1 (15 ounce) can whole kernel corn	425 g
2 carrots, sliced	
1 onion, coarsely chopped	
1 teaspoon dried basil	5 ml
1 teaspoon seasoned salt	5 ml
1 (10 ounce) package frozen broccoli florets	280 g

- Cut potato into 1-inch (2.5 cm) pieces.

- Combine all ingredients except broccoli florets plus 1 teaspoon (5 ml) pepper in sprayed, large slow cooker.

- Cover and cook on LOW for 5 to 6 hours.

- Add broccoli to cooker and cook for additional 1 hour. Serves 4 to 6.

Creamy Ham Chowder

1 (14 ounce) can chicken broth	395 g
1 cup milk	250 ml
1 (10 ounce) can cream of celery soup	280 g
1 (15 ounce) can cream-style corn	425 g
1 (15 ounce) can whole kernel corn	425 g
½ cup dry potato flakes	30 g
1 onion, chopped	
2 - 3 cups cooked, chopped ham	280 - 420 g

- Combine broth, milk, soup, cream-style corn, whole kernel corn, potato flakes, onion and ham in sprayed 6-quart (6 L) slow cooker.

- Cover and cook on LOW for 4 to 5 hours.

- When ready to serve, season with a little salt and pepper. Serves 4 to 6.

Harbor Crab Chowder

2 small zucchini, thinly sliced
1 red bell pepper, seeded, julienned
2 ribs celery, diagonally sliced
1 medium potato, cubed
2 tablespoons butter, melted   30 g
1 (10 ounce) can chicken broth   280 g
1 teaspoon seasoned salt   5 ml
2 tablespoons cornstarch   15 g
3 cups milk   750 ml
2 (6 ounce) cans crabmeat, drained   2 (170 g)
1 (3 ounce) package cream cheese, cubed   85 g

- Place zucchini, bell pepper, celery, potato, butter, broth and seasoned salt in sprayed slow cooker.

- Combine cornstarch and milk in bowl, stir and pour into slow cooker.

- Cover and cook on LOW for 3 to 4 hours.

- Turn heat to HIGH, add crabmeat and cream cheese and stir until cream cheese melts. Serves 4.

Seaside Oyster Chowder

1 small red bell pepper, chopped	
1 onion, chopped	
1 (14 ounce) can chicken broth	425 g
1 medium potato, cubed	
1 fresh jalapeno pepper, seeded, finely chopped	
1 (8 ounce) carton shucked oysters with liquid	230 g
1 (10 ounce) package frozen whole kernel corn, thawed	280 g
1 teaspoon dried oregano	5 ml
½ cup whipping cream	125 ml

- Combine all ingredients except cream in sprayed slow cooker.

- Cover and cook on LOW for 3 to 4 hours.

- When ready to serve, stir in cream. Serves 4.

Country Chowder

1½ pounds boneless, skinless chicken breast halves	680 g
2 tablespoons butter	30 g
2 (10 ounce) cans cream of potato soup	2 (280 g)
1 (14 ounce) can chicken broth	395 g
1 (8 ounce) package frozen whole kernel corn	230 g
1 onion, sliced	
2 ribs celery, sliced	
1 (10 ounce) package frozen peas and carrots, thawed	280 g
½ teaspoon dried thyme leaves	2 ml
½ cup half-and-half cream	125 ml

- Cut chicken into 1-inch (2.5 cm) strips.

- Brown chicken strips in butter in skillet and transfer to sprayed, large slow cooker.

- Add soup, broth, corn, onion, celery, peas and carrots, and thyme and stir.

- Cover and cook on LOW for 3 to 4 hours or until vegetables are tender.

- Turn off heat, stir in half-and-half cream and set aside for about 10 minutes before serving. Serves 4 to 6.

Easy Chowder Chicken

3 cups cooked, cubed chicken	420 g
1 (14 ounce) can chicken broth	395 g
2 (10 ounce) cans cream of potato soup	2 (280 g)
1 large onion, chopped	
3 ribs celery, sliced diagonally	
1 (16 ounce) package frozen whole kernel corn, thawed	455 g
⅔ cup whipping cream	150 ml

- Combine chicken, chicken broth, soup, onion, celery, corn and ¾ cup (175 ml) water in sprayed 5 to 6-quart (5 to 6 L) slow cooker.

- Cover and cook on LOW for 3 to 4 hours.

- Add whipping cream and heat for additional 15 minutes or until thoroughly hot. Serves 4 to 6.

If a slow cooker recipe does not have liquid added, it is probably because the ingredients in the recipe contain enough liquid. If, after cooking, the liquid is too thin or does not have much flavor, remove all the ingredients except the liquid, turn the slow cooker to HIGH and cook until it reduces some. Add about 2 teaspoons (10 ml) flour to liquid and stir well. Continue to cook until it reaches a gravy or sauce consistency and the flour is cooked. Serve on the side.

Down South Jambalaya

3 ribs celery, diagonally sliced
1 onion, chopped
1 red bell pepper, seeded, chopped
1 green bell pepper, seeded, chopped
2 (15 ounce) cans stewed tomatoes   2 (425 g)
2 cups cooked, cubed smoked ham   420 g
½ teaspoon cayenne pepper   2 ml
1 tablespoon dried parsley flakes   15 ml
2 teaspoons minced garlic   10 ml
1 pound peeled, veined shrimp   455 g
Rice, cooked

- Combine celery, onion, bell peppers, tomatoes, ham, cayenne
  pepper, parsley flakes, garlic, and a little salt and pepper in sprayed
  slow cooker.

- Cover and cook on LOW for 7 to 8 hours or on HIGH for 3 to 4 hours.

- Stir in shrimp and cook on LOW 1 hour.

- Serve over rice. Serves 4 to 6.

Bayou Jambalaya

1 pound smoked, cooked sausage links	455 g
1 onion, chopped	
1 green bell pepper, seeded, chopped	
2 teaspoons minced garlic	10 ml
1 (28 ounce) can diced tomatoes	795 g)
1 tablespoon parsley flakes	15 ml
½ teaspoon dried thyme leaves	2 ml
1 teaspoon Cajun seasoning	5 ml
¼ teaspoon cayenne pepper	1 ml
1 pound peeled, veined shrimp	455 g
Rice, cooked	

- Combine all ingredients except shrimp and rice in sprayed slow cooker.

- Cover and cook on LOW for 6 to 8 hours or on HIGH for 3 to 4 hours.

- Stir in shrimp and cook on LOW for additional 1 hour. Serve over rice. Serves 4 to 6.

Jambalaya Cajun

4 chicken breast halves, cubed	
1 (28 ounce) can diced tomatoes	795 g
1 onion, chopped	
1 green bell pepper, chopped	
1 (14 ounce) can chicken broth	395 g
½ cup dry white wine	125 ml
2 teaspoons dried oregano	10 ml
2 teaspoons Cajun seasoning	10 ml
½ teaspoon cayenne pepper	2 ml
1 pound cooked, peeled, veined shrimp	455 g
2 cups cooked rice	315 g

- Place all ingredients except shrimp and rice in sprayed slow cooker and stir.

- Cover and cook on LOW for 6 to 8 hours.

- Turn heat to HIGH, stir in shrimp and rice and cook for additional 15 to 20 minutes. Serves 4 to 6.

Side Dishes

*Pastas, Rice, Potatoes,
Veggies, Beans*

Side Dishes Contents

Creamy Spinach Pasta

1 (12 ounce) package medium egg noodles	340 g
1 cup half-and-half cream	250 ml
1 (10 ounce) package frozen chopped spinach, thawed	280 g
6 tablespoons (¾ stick) butter, melted	90 g
2 teaspoons seasoned salt	10 ml
1½ cups shredded cheddar-Monterey Jack cheese	170 g

- Cook noodles according to package directions and drain.

- Place in sprayed 5 to 6-quart (5 to 6 L) slow cooker. Add half-and-half cream, spinach, butter and seasoned salt and stir until they blend well.

- Cover and cook on LOW for 2 to 3 hours.

- When ready to serve, fold in cheese. Serves 4.

Cheesy Spaghetti Bake

1 (7 ounce) box ready-cut spaghetti	200 g
2 tablespoons butter	30 g
1 (8 ounce) carton sour cream	230 g
1 cup shredded cheddar cheese	115 g
1 (8 ounce) package Monterey Jack cheese, divided	230 g
1 (12 ounce) package frozen, chopped spinach, thawed, very well drained*	340 g
1 (6 ounce) can cheddar french-fried onions, divided	170 g

- Cook spaghetti according to package directions, drain and stir in butter until it melts.

- Combine sour cream, cheddar cheese, half Monterey Jack cheese, spinach and half can onions in large bowl. Fold into spaghetti and spoon into sprayed slow cooker.

- Cover and cook on LOW for 2 to 4 hours.

- When ready to serve, sprinkle remaining Jack cheese and fried onions over top. Serves 4.

TIP: Squeeze spinach between paper towels to completely remove excess moisture.

Crazy Couscous

When rice is boring, try couscous.

1 (10 ounce) box original plain couscous	280 g
2 cups sliced celery	200 g
1 red bell pepper, seeded, chopped	
1 yellow bell pepper, seeded, chopped	
1 (16 ounce) jar creamy alfredo sauce	455 g

- Combine couscous, celery, bell peppers, alfredo sauce and 1½ cups (375 ml) water in sprayed 5-quart (5 L) slow cooker and mix well.

- Cover and cook on LOW for 2 hours, stir once or twice. Check to make sure celery and peppers are cooked, but still crunchy. Serves 4 to 6.

Easy Mixed-up Couscous

1 (5.7 ounce) box herbed-chicken couscous	160 g
1 red bell pepper, seeded, julienned	
1 green bell pepper, seeded, julienned	
2 small yellow squash, sliced	
1 (16 ounce) package frozen mixed vegetables, thawed	455 g
1 (10 ounce) can French onion soup	280 g
¼ cup (½ stick) butter, melted	60 g
½ teaspoon seasoned salt	2 ml

- Combine all ingredients with 1½ cups (375 ml) water in sprayed slow cooker and mix well.

- Cover and cook on LOW for 2 to 4 hours. Serves 4.

Tomato-Green Chile Rice

1½ cups rice	280 g
1 (10 ounce) can diced tomatoes and green chilies	280 g
1 (15 ounce) can stewed tomatoes	425 g
1 (1 ounce) packet taco seasoning	30 g
1 large onion, chopped	

- In 5-quart (5 L) slow cooker, combine all ingredients plus 2 cups (500 ml) water and stir well.

- Cover and cook on LOW for 5 to 7 hours. The flavor will go through the rice better if you stir 2 or 3 times during cooking time. Serves 4.

TIP: Make this "a main dish" by adding 1 pound (455 g) Polish sausage slices to rice mixture.

Quick Risotto

1½ cups Italian risotto (rice)	300 g
3 (14 ounce) cans chicken broth	3 (395 g)
3 tablespoons butter, melted	45 g
1½ cups sliced, fresh mushrooms	110 g
1 cup sliced celery	100 g

- Combine rice, broth, butter, mushrooms and celery in sprayed 4 to 5-quart (4 to 5 L) slow cooker.

- Cover and cook on LOW for 2 to 3 hours or until rice is tender. Serves 4 to 6.

Glazed Sweet Potatoes

3 (15 ounce) cans sweet potatoes, drained	3 (425 g)
¼ cup (½ stick) butter, melted	60 g
2 cups packed brown sugar	440 g
⅓ cup orange juice	75 ml
½ teaspoon ground cinnamon	2 ml

- Cut sweet potatoes into smaller chunks and place in sprayed 4 to 5-quart (4 to 5 L) slow cooker.

- Add butter, brown sugar, orange juice, a little salt and cinnamon and stir well.

- Cover and cook on LOW for 4 to 5 hours. Serves 4 to 6.

Hoppin' John

3 (15 ounce) cans black-eyed peas with liquid	3 (425 g)
1 onion, chopped	
1 (6.2 ounce) package parmesan-butter rice mix	170 g
2 cups cooked, chopped ham	280 g
2 tablespoons butter, melted	30 g

- Combine peas, onion, rice mix, ham, butter and 1¾ cups (425 ml) water in sprayed slow cooker and mix well.

- Cover and cook on LOW for 2 to 4 hours. Serves 6 to 8.

Fun Sweet Potatoes Hawaiian

3 (15 ounce) cans sweet potatoes, drained	3 (425 g)
½ (20 ounce) can pineapple pie filling	½ (570 g)
2 tablespoons butter, melted	30 g
½ cup packed brown sugar	110 g
½ teaspoon ground cinnamon	2 ml

- Place sweet potatoes, pie filling, melted butter, brown sugar and cinnamon in sprayed 4 to 5-quart (4 to 5 L) slow cooker and lightly stir.

- Cover and cook on LOW for 2 to 3 hours.

Topping:

1 cup packed light brown sugar	220 g
3 tablespoons butter, melted	45 g
½ cup flour	60 g
1 cup coarsely chopped nuts	170 g

- Preheat oven to 350° (175° C).

- While potatoes cook, combine topping ingredients in bowl, spread out on foil-lined baking pan and bake for 15 to 20 minutes.

- When ready to serve, sprinkle topping over sweet potatoes. Serves 6 to 8.

Cheesy Potato Blend

1 (28 ounce) bag frozen diced potatoes with onions and peppers, thawed	795 g
1 (8 ounce) package shredded Monterey Jack and cheddar cheese blend	230 g
1 (10 ounce) can cream of celery soup	280 g
1 (8 ounce) carton sour cream	230 g

- Combine potatoes, cheese, soup, sour cream and 1 teaspoon (5 ml) pepper in sprayed 5 to 6-quart (5 to 6 L) slow cooker and mix well.

- Cover and cook on LOW 4 to 6 hours. Stir well before serving. Serves 6 to 8.

New Potato Fiesta

2½ pounds new (red) potatoes with skins, quartered   1.1 kg
1 onion, cut into 8 parts
1 (10 ounce) can fiesta nacho cheese soup   280 g
1 (8 ounce) carton sour cream   230 g
1 (1 ounce) packet ranch salad dressing mix   30 g
Chopped fresh parsley

- Place potatoes and onion in sprayed 4 to 5-quart (4 to 5 L) slow cooker.

- Combine, soup, sour cream and dressing mix in bowl and whisk well to mix. Add to slow cooker

- Cover and cook on LOW for 6 to 7 hours.

- To serve, sprinkle chopped fresh parsley over potato mixture. Serves 4 to 6.

Creamy New Potatoes

2 - 2½ pounds new potatoes with peels, quartered	910 g - 1.1 kg
1 (8 ounce) package cream cheese, softened	230 g
1 (10 ounce) can fiesta nacho soup	280 g
1 (1 ounce) packet buttermilk ranch dressing mix	30 g
1 cup milk	250 ml

- Place potatoes in sprayed 6-quart (6 L) slow cooker.

- Beat cream cheese in bowl until creamy and fold in soup, ranch salad dressing mix and milk. Stir into potatoes.

- Cover and cook on LOW for 3 to 4 hours or until potatoes are well done. Serves 4 to 6.

Potato Fancy

1 (5 ounce) box scalloped potatoes	145 g
1 (5 ounce) box au gratin potatoes	145 g
1 cup milk	250 ml
6 tablespoons (¾ stick) butter, melted	90 g
½ pound bacon, cooked crisp, crumbled	230 g

- Place all potatoes in sprayed slow cooker.

- Combine milk, butter and 4¼ cups (1 L) water in bowl and pour over potatoes.

- Cover and cook on LOW for 4 to 5 hours.

- When ready to serve, sprinkle crumbled bacon over top of potatoes. Serves 4 to 6.

Yummy Ham and Hash Browns

1 (26 ounce) package frozen hash-brown potatoes
   with onions and peppers   740 g
2 - 3 cups cooked, chopped ham   280 - 420 g
1 (16 ounce) carton sour cream   455 g
1 (8 ounce) package shredded cheddar Jack cheese   230 g
1 (3 ounce) can french-fried onions   85 g

- Cook potatoes in a little oil in large skillet. Transfer to sprayed 5 to 6-quart (5 L) slow cooker.

- Combine ham, sour cream and cheese in bowl and mix into potatoes.

- Cover and cook on LOW for 2 to 3 hours.

- Dress up potatoes by sprinkling french-fried onions on top. Serves 4 to 6.

*Casseroles, soups and stews can easily be adapted to the
slow cooker method. You may not need as much liquid
(unless cooking rice or pasta) because slow cookers retain the
moisture in the ingredients, unlike more conventional methods.*

Easy Baked Potatoes

10 medium russet potatoes with peels
¼ - ½ cup canola oil 60 - 125 ml
Butter
Sour cream

- Pierce potatoes with fork. Brush potato skins with oil and sprinkle salt and pepper on potato skins. Wrap potatoes individually in foil and place in large slow cooker.

- Cover and cook on LOW for 7 to 8 hours or until potatoes are tender.

- Serve with butter, sour cream and assorted toppings such as: shredded cheese, salsa, ranch dip, chopped green onions, bacon bits, chopped boiled eggs, cheese-hamburger dip, broccoli-cheese soup, etc. Serves 4.

Potato Know-How

1 (10 ounce) can cream of chicken soup	280 g
1 (8 ounce) carton sour cream	230 g
2 pounds potatoes, peeled, cubed	910 g
1 (8 ounce) package shredded cheddar Jack cheese	230 g
1 cup crushed potato chips	55 g

- Combine soup, sour cream, some salt and pepper and ¼ cup (60 ml) water in bowl.

- Combine potatoes and cheese in sprayed 5-quart (5 L) slow cooker. Spoon soup-sour cream mixture over potatoes.

- Cover and cook on LOW for 8 to 9 hours.

- When ready to serve, sprinkle crushed potato chips over potatoes. Serves 4 to 6.

Fantastic Cheesy Potatoes

1 (28 ounce) package frozen hash-brown potatoes with onions and peppers, thawed	75 g
2 (10 ounce) cans cream of chicken soup	2 (280 g)
1 (8 ounce) carton sour cream	230 g
½ cup (1 stick) butter, melted, divided	115 g
1 (8 ounce) package shredded cheddar cheese	230 g
2 tablespoons dried parsley	5 g
2 cups dry stuffing mix	100 g

- Combine potatoes, soup, sour cream, ¼ cup (60 g) melted butter, cheese, parsley and 1 teaspoon (5 ml) salt in large bowl and mix well.

- Spoon mixture into sprayed, large slow cooker. Sprinkle stuffing mix over potato mixture and drizzle remaining butter over stuffing.

- Cover and cook on LOW for 7 to 9 hours or on HIGH for 3 to 4 hours. Serves 4 to 6.

Buttered New Potatoes

18 - 20 new (red) potatoes with peels	
¼ cup (½ stick) butter, melted	**60 g**
1 tablespoon dried parsley	**15 ml**
½ teaspoon garlic powder	**2 ml**
½ teaspoon paprika	**2 ml**

- Combine all ingredients plus ½ teaspoon (2 ml) each of salt and pepper in sprayed slow cooker and mix well.

- Cover and cook on LOW for 7 hours or on HIGH for 3 hours 30 minutes to 4 hours.

- When ready to serve, remove potatoes with slotted spoon to serving dish and cover to keep warm.

- Add about 2 tablespoons (30 ml) water to drippings and stir until they blend well.

- Pour mixture over potatoes. Serves 4 to 6.

Ranch New Potatoes

2 pounds new (red) potatoes with peels, quartered	**910 g**
¼ cup canola oil	**60 ml**
1 (1 ounce) packet ranch dressing mix	**30 g**
¼ cup chopped fresh parsley	**15 g**

- Place potatoes, oil, dressing mix and ¼ cup (60 ml) water in sprayed 4 to 5-quart (4 to 5L) slow cooker and toss to coat potatoes.

- Cover and cook on LOW for 3 to 4 hours or until potatoes are tender. When ready to serve, sprinkle parsley over potatoes and toss. Serves 4 to 6.

Loaded Potatoes

6 medium potatoes, peeled	
1 (8 ounce) package shredded cheddar cheese, divided	**230 g**
1 (10 ounce) can cream of chicken soup	**280 g**
¼ cup (½ stick) butter, melted	**60 g**
1 (8 ounce) carton sour cream	**230 g**
1 (3 ounce) can french-fried onions	**85 g**

- Cut potatoes in 1-inch (2.5 cm) strips. Toss potatoes with some salt and pepper plus half cheese in bowl. Place in sprayed slow cooker. Combine soup, melted butter and 2 tablespoons (30 ml) water in saucepan and heat just enough to pour over potato mixture.

- Cover and cook on LOW for 6 to 8 hours or until potatoes are tender.

- Stir in sour cream and remaining cheese. When ready to serve, sprinkle onion rings over top of potatoes. Serves 4 to 6.

Cauliflower-Squash

1 (16 ounce) package frozen cauliflower florets, thawed	455 g
1 (15 ounce) can whole kernel corn	425 g
¾ pound small yellow squash, chopped	340 g
¼ cup (½ stick) butter, melted	60 g
2 (10 ounce) cans cheddar cheese soup	2 (280 g)
6 slices bacon, cooked, crumbled	

- Place cauliflower, corn and squash in sprayed slow cooker and sprinkle with a little salt and pepper.

- Pour melted butter over vegetables and spoon cheese soup on top. Sprinkle with crumbled bacon.

- Cover and cook on LOW for 4 to 5 hours. Serves 4 to 6.

Green Veggie Mix

1 (10 ounce) package frozen broccoli florets, thawed	280 g
1 (10 ounce) package frozen cauliflower, thawed	280 g
1 (10 ounce) package frozen brussels sprouts	280 g
4 small yellow squash, sliced	
1 (10 ounce) can cream of mushroom soup	280 g
1 (16 ounce) package cubed Velveeta® cheese	455 g

- Place vegetables in sprayed slow cooker.

- Layer soup and cheese on top of vegetables.

- Cover and cook on LOW for 3 to 4 hours. Serves 4 to 6.

Vegetable-Rice Mix

1 (16 ounce) package frozen vegetable mix, thawed	455 g
1 (10 ounce) package frozen green peas, thawed	280 g
1 (10 ounce) package frozen whole kernel corn, thawed	280 g
2 (10 ounce) cans cream of mushroom soup	2 (280 g)
1 cup instant white rice	95 g
1 (8 ounce) carton cubed Velveeta® cheese	230 g
1 cup milk	250 ml
2 tablespoons butter, melted	30 g
1 teaspoon seasoned salt	5 ml

- Place all vegetables in large, sprayed slow cooker.

- Combine soup, rice, cheese, milk, butter, seasoned salt and 1 cup (250 ml) water in saucepan, heat just enough to mix and pour over vegetables.

- Cover and cook on LOW for 4 to 5 hours. Stir before serving. Serves 6 to 8.

Cheesy Spinach Surprise

1 (10 ounce) package frozen chopped spinach, thawed, drained 280 g
1 (16 ounce) package frozen chopped spinach, thawed, drained 455 g
1 (8 ounce) package cream cheese, cubed, softened   230 g
1 (10 ounce) can cream of chicken soup   280 g
1 egg, beaten
1 (8 ounce) package shredded cheddar cheese   230 g

- Squeeze spinach between paper towels to completely remove excess moisture.

- Combine spinach, cream cheese, chicken soup, egg and a little salt and pepper in bowl. Spoon into sprayed slow cooker.

- Cover and cook on LOW for 3 to 4 hours.

- Before serving, stir in cheddar cheese. Serves 4 to 6.

Simple Veggie Cook

1 (16 ounce) package frozen broccoli, cauliflower and carrots   455 g
2 medium zucchini, halved lengthwise, sliced
1 (1 ounce) packet ranch dressing mix   30 g
2 tablespoons butter, melted   30 g

- Place broccoli, cauliflower and carrots and zucchini in sprayed 4-quart (4 L) slow cooker.

- Combine ranch dressing mix, melted butter and ½ cup (125 ml) water in bowl, spoon over vegetables and stir.

- Cover and cook on LOW for 2 to 3 hours. Serves 4.

Creamy Spinach

2 (10 ounce) packages frozen chopped spinach, thawed, drained	280 g
1 (16 ounce) carton small curd cottage cheese	455 g
1½ cups shredded American or cheddar cheese	175 g
3 eggs, beaten	
¼ cup (½ stick) butter, melted	60 g
¼ cup flour	30 g

- Squeeze spinach between paper towels to completely remove excess moisture..

- Combine all ingredients in bowl and mix well. Spoon into sprayed slow cooker.

- Cover and cook on HIGH for 1 hour, change heat to LOW and cook for additional 3 to 5 hours or until knife inserted in center comes out clean. Serves 4 to 6.

Creamy Peas and Potatoes

2 pounds small new (red) potatoes with peels, quartered	910 g
1 (16 ounce) package frozen green peas with pearl onions, thawed	455 g
2 (10 ounce) cans fiesta nacho cheese soup	2 (280 g)
½ cup milk	125 ml

- Sprinkle potatoes with a little salt and pepper, place in sprayed slow cooker and place peas on top. Combine soup and milk in saucepan, heat just enough to mix well and spoon over peas.

- Cover and cook on LOW for 4 to 5 hours. Serves 6 to 8.

Super Supper Corn

2 (15 ounce) cans whole kernel corn	2 (425 g)
2 (15 ounce) cans creamed corn	2 (425 g)
½ cup (1 stick) butter, melted	115 g
1 (8 ounce) carton sour cream	230 g
1 (8 ounce) package jalapeno cornbread mix	230 g

- Combine all ingredients in large bowl and mix well.

- Pour into sprayed slow cooker, cover and cook on LOW for 4 to 5 hours. Serves 6 to 8.

TIP: Make this a one-dish meal by adding 2 to 3 cups (280 to 420 g) cubed ham.

Quick-Fix Corn

1 (3 ounce) package cream cheese	85 g
1 (8 ounce) package cream cheese	230 g
½ cup (1 stick) butter	115 g
2 (16 ounce) packages frozen whole kernel corn, thawed	2 (455 g)

- Combine cream cheese and butter in sprayed 4-quart (4 L) slow cooker.

- Cook on HIGH and stir just until cheese and butter melt. Add corn and ½ teaspoon (2 ml) pepper and a little salt.

- Cover and cook on LOW for 1 hour 30 minutes to 2 hours. Serves 4 to 6.

Squash Delight

1 pound yellow squash, thinly sliced	455 g
1 pound zucchini, thinly sliced	455 g
3 ribs celery, sliced	
1 onion, chopped	
1 (10 ounce) can cream of chicken soup	280 g
1 (8 ounce) carton sour cream	230 g
3 tablespoons flour	20 g
1 (6 ounce) package seasoned stuffing mix	170 g
½ cup (1 stick) butter, melted	115 g

- Combine squash, zucchini, celery, onion and soup in large bowl.

- In separate bowl, mix sour cream with flour and stir into vegetables.

- Toss stuffing with melted butter and spoon half into sprayed slow cooker.

- Top with vegetables and spoon remaining stuffing on top.

- Cover and cook on LOW for 5 to 7 hours. Serves 6 to 8.

Sunshine Squash

2 pounds medium yellow squash, sliced	910 g
2 onions, coarsely chopped	
3 ribs celery, diagonally sliced	
1 green bell pepper, seeded, julienned	
1 (8 ounce) package cream cheese, cubed	230 g
1 teaspoon sugar	5 ml
¼ cup (½ stick) butter, melted	60 g
1 (10 ounce) can cheddar cheese soup	280 g
1½ cups seasoned breadcrumbs	180 g

- Combine all ingredients, except breadcrumbs in sprayed slow cooker and mix well with 1 teaspoon (5 ml) each of salt and pepper.

- Cover and cook on LOW for 3 to 4 hours. Before serving, sprinkle top with breadcrumbs. Serves 6 to 8.

TIP: If you don't like black specks, use white pepper instead of black pepper.

Krazy Karrots

1 (16 ounce) package baby carrots	455 g
¼ cup (½ stick) butter, melted	60 g
⅔ cup packed brown sugar	150 g
1 (1 ounce) packet ranch dressing mix	30 g

- Combine carrots, butter, brown sugar, ranch dressing mix and ¼ cup (60 ml) water in sprayed 4-quart (4 L) slow cooker and stir well.

- Cover and cook on low for 3 to 4 hours and stir occasionally. Serves 4.

Easy Squash Fix

1½ pounds small yellow squash	680 g
1½ pounds zucchini	680 g
¼ cup (½ stick) butter, melted	60 g
½ cup seasoned breadcrumbs	60 g
½ cup shredded cheddar cheese	60 g

- Cut yellow squash and zucchini in small pieces.

- Place in sprayed slow cooker and sprinkle with a little salt and pepper.

- Pour butter over squash and sprinkle with breadcrumbs and cheese.

- Cover and cook on LOW for 5 to 6 hours. Serves 6 to 8.

Slow cookers usually have two temperature settings: LOW and HIGH. LOW is about 200° (95° C) and HIGH is about 300° (150° C). When the heating elements are in the sides as well as the bottom, food does not have to be stirred. When the heating element is in the bottom only, it is best to stir the food once or twice. Increase cooking time by 15 to 20 minutes each time the lid is removed.

Sugared-Cinnamon Carrots

2 (16 ounce) packages baby carrots	2 (455 g)
¾ cup packed brown sugar	165 g
¼ cup honey	85 g
½ cup orange juice	125 ml
2 tablespoons butter, melted	30 g
¾ teaspoon ground cinnamon	4 ml

- Place carrots in sprayed 3 to 4-quart (3 to 4 L) slow cooker.

- Combine brown sugar, honey, orange juice, butter and cinnamon in bowl and mix well.

- Pour over carrots and mix so sugar-cinnamon mixture coats carrots.

- Cover and cook on LOW for 3 hours 30 minutes to 4 hours and stir twice during cooking time.

- About 20 minutes before serving, transfer carrots with slotted spoon to serving dish and cover to keep warm.

- Pour liquid from cooker into saucepan; boil for several minutes until liquid reduces by half. Spoon over carrots in serving dish.
  Serves 6 to 8.

Black Beans and Rice

1 pound dry black or kidney beans	**455 g**
2 onions, chopped	
2 teaspoons minced garlic	**10 ml**
1 tablespoon ground cumin	**15 ml**
1 (14 ounce) can chicken broth	**395 g**
1 cup instant brown rice	**190 g**

- Place beans in saucepan, cover with water and soak overnight.

- Drain and rinse beans and combine with onion, garlic, cumin, chicken broth, 2 teaspoons (10 ml) salt and 2 cups (500 ml) water in sprayed 4 to 5-quart (4 to 5 L) slow cooker.

- Cover and cook on LOW for 4 to 6 hours.

- Stir in instant rice, cover and cook for additional 20 minutes. Serves 4 to 6.

TIP: If soaking beans overnight is not an option, place beans in saucepan and add enough water to cover by 2 inches (5 cm). Bring to a boil, reduce heat and simmer for 10 minutes. Let stand 1 hour, drain and rinse beans.

Trail Drive Frijoles

2 cups dry pinto beans	400 g
2 onions, finely chopped	
2 tablespoons chili powder	15 g
1 teaspoon minced garlic	5 ml
1 (15 ounce) can tomato sauce	425 g
1½ pounds lean ground beef	680 g

- Place beans in large saucepan and cover with water. Bring to a boil, turn off heat and let stand for 1 hour.

- Drain and transfer beans to sprayed, large slow cooker. Add onions, chili powder, garlic, tomato sauce, 1 tablespoon (15 ml) salt and 8 cups (1.9 L) water.

- Brown ground beef in skillet, drain and transfer to cooker.

- Cover and cook on LOW for 8 to 9 hours or until beans are tender; stir occasionally. Serves 6 to 8.

Creamy Limas

2 (16 ounce) packages frozen baby lima beans, thawed	2 (455 g)
1 (10 ounce) can cream of celery soup	280 g
1 (10 ounce) can cream of onion soup	280 g
1 red bell pepper, seeded, julienned	
1 (4 ounce) jar sliced mushrooms, drained	115 g
¼ cup milk	60 ml
1 cup shredded cheddar-colby cheese	115 g

- Combine lima beans, soups, bell pepper, mushrooms and ½ teaspoon (2 ml) salt in saucepan and heat just enough to mix well.

- Pour into sprayed 4 to 6-quart (4 to 6 L) slow cooker.

- Cover and cook on LOW for 8 to 9 hours.

- Just before serving, stir in milk, remove to serving bowl and sprinkle cheese over top. Serves 6 to 8.

Slow cooking retains most of the moisture in food; if there is too much liquid at the end of cooking time, remove cover, increase heat to HIGH and cook uncovered for an additional 45 minutes.

5-Bean Bake

4 thick slices bacon, cooked crisp, crumbled	
1 (15 ounce) can kidney beans, drained	425 g
1 (15 ounce) can lima beans with liquid	425 g
1 (15 ounce) can pinto beans with liquid	425 g
1 (15 ounce) can navy beans with liquid	425 g
1 (15 ounce) can pork and beans with liquid	425 g
1 onion, chopped	
¾ cup chili sauce	205 g
1 cup packed brown sugar	220 g
1 tablespoon Worcestershire sauce	15 ml

• Combine all ingredients in sprayed slow cooker and mix well.

• Cover and cook on LOW for 5 to 6 hours. Serves 6 to 8.

Better Butter Beans

2 cups sliced celery	200 g
2 onions, chopped	
1 green bell pepper, seeded, julienned	
1 (15 ounce) can stewed tomatoes	425 g
¼ cup (½ stick) butter, melted	60 g
1 tablespoon chicken seasoning	15 ml
3 (15 ounce) cans butter beans, drained	3 (425 g)

• Combine all ingredients in sprayed slow cooker and mix well.

• Cover and cook on LOW for 3 to 4 hours. Serves 6 to 8.

Green Bean Crunch

2 (16 ounce) packages frozen whole green beans, thawed	2 (455 g)
3 ribs celery, diagonally sliced	
1 red bell pepper, seeded, julienned	
2 (11 ounce) cans sliced water chestnuts, drained	2 (310 g)
1 (10 ounce) can cream of chicken soup	280 g
½ cup slivered almonds	85 g
1 (3 ounce) can french-fried onions	85 g

- Combine green beans, celery, bell pepper, water chestnuts, chicken soup and almonds in sprayed slow cooker.

- Cover and cook on LOW for 2 to 4 hours. About 10 minutes before serving, top with french-fried onions. Serves 6 to 8.

Big Bean Bowl

3 (15 ounce) cans black beans, rinsed, drained	3 (425 g)
3 (15 ounce) cans great northern beans, rinsed, drained	3 (425 g)
1 (16 ounce) jar hot, thick-and-chunky salsa	455 g
½ cup packed brown sugar	110 g

- Combine black beans, great northern beans, salsa and brown sugar in sprayed 5 to 6-quart (5 L) slow cooker.

- Cover and cook on LOW for 3 to 4 hours. Serves 6 to 8.

TIP: *To include pinto beans in this dish, substitute 1 can pinto beans for 1 of the cans of black beans.*

Green Beans Zip

2 (16 ounce) packages frozen whole green beans, thawed	2 (425 g)
2 (8 ounce) cans sliced water chestnuts, drained	2 (230 g)
1 (16 ounce) package cubed jalapeno Velveeta® cheese	425 g
1 (10 ounce) can diced tomatoes and green chilies	280 g
¼ cup (½ stick) butter, melted	60 g
1 tablespoon chicken seasoning	15 ml
1½ cups slightly crushed potato chips	85 g

- Combine green beans, water chestnuts, cheese, tomatoes and green chilies, melted butter, and seasoning in sprayed slow cooker and mix well.

- Cover and cook on LOW for 3 to 5 hours. Just before serving, cover top with crushed potato chips. Serves 6 to 8.

TIP: If you would like this to be a one-dish meal, add 2 to 3 cups (280 to 420 g) cooked, cubed ham.

Crunchy Green Bean Bite

2 (16 ounce) packages frozen whole green beans, thawed	2 (455 g)
2 (10 ounce) cans fiesta nacho cheese soup	2 (280 g)
1 (8 ounce) package seasoning blend (onions and bell peppers)	230 g
1 (8 ounce) can sliced water chestnuts, halved	230 g
1 teaspoon seasoned salt	5 ml

- Combine all ingredients plus ¼ cup (60 ml) water in sprayed, large slow cooker and stir to mix well.

- Cover and cook on LOW for 4 to 5 hours. Serves 6 to 8.

Mom's Fresh Green Beans

2 pounds fresh green beans   910 g
1 onion, finely chopped
4 slices thick bacon
5 - 6 medium new (red) potatoes
1 teaspoon sugar   5 ml

- Snap and wash green beans, place beans and onion in sprayed
  5 to 6-quart (5 to 6 L) slow cooker.

- Cut bacon in 1-inch (2.5 cm) pieces and fry in skillet until crisp.

- Remove some of deeper "eyes" in new potatoes and cut into quarters.

- Add cooked bacon pieces, potatoes and 1 cup (250 ml) water to cooker.

- Add about 1½ teaspoons (7 ml) salt and sugar. (A touch of sugar
  always intensifies flavor in fresh vegetables.)

- Cover and cook on LOW for 3 to 4 hours. Serves 6 to 8.

*Fill a slow cooker with a breakfast casserole recipe
and let it cook overnight for a wonderful morning meal.*

Creamy Beans & Potatoes

6 - 8 medium new (red) potatoes with peels, sliced	
5 cups fresh whole green beans, trimmed	550 g
2 tablespoons dry minced onions	30 ml
¼ cup (½ stick) butter, melted	60 g
1 (10 ounce) can cream of celery soup	280 g
1 (10 ounce) can fiesta nacho cheese soup	280 g

- Place potatoes, green beans and minced onions in sprayed slow cooker.

- Pour melted butter over vegetables.

- Combine soups and ⅓ cup (75 ml) water in saucepan. Heat just enough to be able to mix soups and pour over vegetables.

- Cover and cook on LOW for 7 to 8 hours. Serves 6 to 8.

Broccoli-Cauliflower Mix

1 (16 ounce) package frozen broccoli florets, thawed	455 g
1 (16 ounce) package frozen cauliflower florets, thawed	455 g
2 (10 ounce) cans nacho cheese soup	2 (280 g)
6 slices bacon, cooked, crumbled	

- Place broccoli and cauliflower in sprayed slow cooker.

- Sprinkle with a little salt and pepper.

- Spoon soup over top and sprinkle with bacon.

- Cover and cook on LOW for 3 to 4 hours. Serves 6 to 8.

Easy Company Broccoli

1½ pounds fresh broccoli, trimmed well	680 g
1 (10 ounce) can cream of chicken soup	280 g
½ cup mayonnaise	110 g
1 (8 ounce) package shredded cheddar cheese, divided	230 g
¼ cup slivered almonds, toasted	40 g

- Place broccoli in sprayed slow cooker.

- Combine chicken soup, mayonnaise, half cheese and ¼ cup (60 ml) water in bowl. Spoon over broccoli.

- Cover and cook on LOW 2 to 3 hours. When ready to serve, sprinkle remaining cheese over broccoli and top with almonds. Serves 6 to 8.

Easy Broccoli Casserole

¼ cup (½ stick) butter, melted	60 g
1 (10 ounce) can cream of mushroom soup	280 g
1 (10 ounce) can cream of onion soup	280 g
1 cup instant rice	95 g
1 (8 ounce) package cubed Velveeta® cheese	230 g
2 (10 ounce) packages frozen chopped broccoli, thawed	2 (280 g)

- Combine all ingredients, plus ½ cup (125 ml) water in sprayed slow cooker and stir well.

- Cover and cook on HIGH for 2 to 3 hours. Serves 4 to 6.

Veggie-Cheese Dish

2 (16 ounce) packages frozen broccoli florets, thawed,
   stems removed   2 (425 g)
2 (15 ounce) cans whole new potatoes, drained   2 (425 g)
2 (10 ounce) cans cream of celery soup   2 (280 g)
½ cup milk   125 ml
1 (8 ounce) package shredded cheddar cheese, divided   230 g
1½ cups cracker crumbs, divided   90 g

- Combine broccoli and potatoes in sprayed slow cooker.

- Combine soup and milk in saucepan; heat just enough to mix well and pour over broccoli and potatoes.

- Sprinkle half cheese and half crumbs over broccoli.

- Cover and cook on LOW for 3 to 4 hours.

- When ready to serve, sprinkle remaining cheese and crumbs over top. Serves 6 to 8.

Chicken Main Dishes

Southwestern, Italian, Country, Southern

Chicken Main Dishes Contents

Chicken Main Dishes Contents

If you have meat cooking in the slow cooker while you are away and the power goes out, throw the food away even if it looks done. If you are at home when the power goes out, finish cooking on a gas range or grill. If the food is completely cooked in the slow cooker, it will stay safe for about 2 hours, then it should be refrigerated.

Asparagus Dinner Chicken

8 - 10 boneless, skinless chicken thighs	
2 tablespoons butter	**30 g**
1 (10 ounce) can cream of celery soup	**280 g**
1 (10 ounce) can cheddar cheese soup	**280 g**
⅓ cup milk	**75 ml**
1 (16 ounce) package frozen asparagus cuts	**455 g**

- Place chicken thighs in sprayed 5-quart (5 L) slow cooker. Combine butter, soups and milk in saucepan. Heat just enough for butter to melt and mix well. Pour over chicken thighs.

- Cover and cook on LOW for 5 to 6 hours. Remove cover, place asparagus cuts over chicken and cook for additional 1 hour. Serves 4 to 6.

Arroz con Pollo

3 pounds chicken thighs	**1.4 kg**
2 (15 ounce) cans Italian stewed tomatoes	**2 (425 g)**
1 (16 ounce) package frozen green peas, thawed	**455 g**
2 cups rice	**370 g**
1 (.28 ounce) packet yellow rice seasoning mix	**10 g**
2 (14 ounce) cans chicken broth	**2 (395 g)**
1 heaping teaspoon minced garlic	**5 ml**
1 teaspoon dried oregano	**5 ml**

- Combine all ingredients plus ¾ cup (175 ml) water in sprayed, large slow cooker and stir well.

- Cover and cook on LOW for 7 to 8 hours or on HIGH for 3 hours 30 minutes to 4 hours. Serves 6 to 8.

Seasoned Italian Chicken

1 small head cabbage	
1 onion	
1 (4 ounce) jar sliced mushrooms, drained	115 g
1 medium zucchini, sliced	
1 red bell pepper, seeded, julienned	
1 teaspoon Italian seasoning	5 ml
1½ pounds boneless, skinless chicken thighs	680 g
2 (15 ounce) cans Italian stewed tomatoes	2 (425 g)
1 teaspoon minced garlic	5 ml

- Cut cabbage into wedges, slice onion and separate into rings.

- Make layers of cabbage, onion, mushrooms, zucchini and bell pepper in sprayed 6-quart (6 L) slow cooker.

- Sprinkle Italian seasoning over vegetables. Place chicken thighs on top of vegetables.

- Mix tomatoes with garlic and pour over chicken.

- Cover and cook on LOW for 4 to 6 hours. Serves 4 to 6.

TIP: When serving, sprinkle a little parmesan cheese over each serving.

Basic Down Home Chicken

1 cup half-and-half cream	250 ml
1 tablespoon flour	15 ml
1 (1 ounce) packet chicken gravy mix	30 g
1 pound boneless, skinless chicken thighs	455 g
1 (16 ounce) package frozen stew vegetables, thawed	455 g
1 (4 ounce) jar sliced mushrooms, drained	115 g
1 (10 ounce) package frozen green peas, thawed	280 g
1½ cups biscuit mix	180 g
1 bunch green onions, chopped	
½ cup milk	125 ml

- Combine half-and-half cream, flour, gravy mix and 1 cup (250 ml) water in bowl, stir until smooth and pour in sprayed, large slow cooker.

- Cut chicken into 1-inch (2.5 cm) pieces and stir in vegetables and mushrooms.

- Cover and cook on LOW for 4 to 6 hours or until chicken is tender and sauce thickens. Stir in peas.

- Combine baking mix, onions and milk in bowl and mix well.

- Drop tablespoonfuls of dough onto chicken mixture.

- Change heat to HIGH, cover and cook for additional 50 to 60 minutes. Serves 4 to 6.

Chili Sauce Chicken

2 pounds chicken thighs	910 g
¾ cup chili sauce	205 g
¾ cup packed brown sugar	165 g
1 (1 ounce) packet onion soup mix	30 g
⅛ teaspoon cayenne pepper	.5 ml
Rice, cooked	

- Spray 5-quart (5 L) slow cooker and arrange chicken pieces in sprayed 5-quart (5 L) slow cooker.

- Combine chili sauce, brown sugar, onion soup mix, cayenne pepper and ¼ cup (60 ml) water in bowl and spoon over chicken.

- Cover and cook on LOW for 6 to 7 hours. Serve over rice. Serves 4 to 6.

Maple-Plum Glazed Turkey Breast

1 cup red plum jam	320 g
1 cup maple syrup	250 ml
1 teaspoon dry mustard	5 ml
¼ cup lemon juice	60 ml
1 (3 - 5 pound) bone-in turkey breast	1.4 - 2.3 kg

- Combine jam, syrup, mustard and lemon juice in saucepan. Bring to a boil, turn heat down and simmer for about 20 minutes or until slightly thick. Set aside 1 cup (250 ml). Place turkey breast in sprayed slow cooker and pour remaining glaze over turkey.

- Cover and cook on LOW for 5 to 7 hours.

- When ready to serve, slice turkey and serve with heated remaining glaze. Serves 6 to 8.

Chicken Alfredo

1½ pounds boneless, skinless chicken thighs, cut into strips	680 g
2 ribs celery, sliced diagonally	
1 red bell pepper, seeded, julienned	
1 (16 ounce) jar alfredo sauce	455 g
3 cups fresh broccoli florets	215 g
1 (8 ounce) package fettuccini or linguine	230 g
1 (4 ounce) package shredded parmesan cheese	115 g

- Layer chicken, celery and bell pepper in sprayed 4 to 5-quart (4 to 5 L) slow cooker.

- Pour alfredo sauce evenly over vegetables.

- Cover and cook on LOW for 5 to 6 hours.

- About 30 minutes before serving, turn heat to HIGH and add broccoli florets to chicken-alfredo mixture.

- Cover and cook for additional 30 minutes.

- Cook pasta according to package directions and drain.

- Just before serving pour pasta into cooker, mix well and sprinkle parmesan cheese on top. Serves 4 to 6.

Chicken-Stuffing Time

1 (10 ounce) can cream of chicken soup	280 g
2 ribs celery, sliced	
½ cup (1 stick) butter, melted	115 g
3 cups cooked, cubed chicken	420 g
1 (16 ounce) package frozen broccoli, corn and red peppers	455 g
1 (8 ounce) box cornbread stuffing mix	230 g

- Combine chicken soup, celery, butter, chicken, vegetables, stuffing mix and ⅓ cup (75 ml) water in large bowl. Mix well and transfer to 5 or 6-quart (5 to 6 L) slow cooker.

- Cover and cook on LOW for 5 to 6 hours. Serves 4 to 6.

Holiday-Any-Day Chicken

2 (10 ounce) cans cream of chicken soup	2 (280 g)
⅓ cup (⅔ stick) butter, melted	75 g
3 cups cooked, cubed chicken	420 g
1 (16 ounce) package frozen broccoli, corn and red peppers	455 g
1 (10 ounce) package frozen green peas	280 g
1 (8 ounce) package cornbread stuffing mix	230 g

- Combine soup, melted butter and ⅓ cup (75 ml) water in bowl and mix well. Add chicken, vegetables and stuffing mix and stir well. Spoon mixture into sprayed large slow cooker.

- Cover and cook on LOW for 5 to 6 hours or on HIGH for 2 hours 30 minutes to 3 hours. Serves 4 to 6.

El Paso Slow Chicken

6 (6 inch) corn tortillas	6 (15 cm)
3 cups cooked, cubed chicken	420 g
1 (10 ounce) package frozen whole kernel corn	280 g
1 (15 ounce) can pinto beans with liquid	425 g
1 (16 ounce) hot jar salsa	455 g
¼ cup sour cream	60 g
1 tablespoon flour	15 ml
3 tablespoons snipped fresh cilantro	5 g
1 (8 ounce) package shredded 4-cheese blend	230 g

- Preheat oven to 250° (121° C).

- Cut tortillas into 6 wedges. Place half wedges on baking pan, bake for about 10 minutes and set aside.

- Place remaining tortilla wedges in sprayed slow cooker.

- Layer chicken, corn and beans over tortillas in cooker.

- Combine salsa, sour cream, flour and cilantro in bowl and pour over corn and beans.

- Cover and cook on LOW for 3 to 4 hours.

- When ready to serve, place baked tortillas wedges and cheese on top of each serving. Serves 4 to 6.

Simple Chicken Cacciatore

2 onions, thinly sliced	
1 (2½ - 3) pound fryer chicken, quartered	1.1 - 1.4 kg
2 (6 ounce) cans tomato paste	2 (170 g)
1 (4 ounce) can sliced mushrooms	115 g
1½ teaspoons minced garlic	7 ml
½ teaspoon dried basil	2 ml
2 teaspoons oregano leaves	10 ml
⅔ cup dry white wine	150 ml

- Place sliced onions in sprayed, oval slow cooker.

- Wash and dry chicken quarters with paper towels. Place in slow cooker.

- Combine tomato paste, mushrooms, garlic, basil, oregano and wine in bowl and pour over chicken quarters.

- Cover and cook on LOW for 7 to 8 hours or on HIGH for 4 hours. Serves 4 to 6.

Easy Coq au Vin

1 large fryer chicken, quartered, skinned
Canola oil
10 - 12 small white onions, peeled
½ pound whole mushrooms   230 g
1 teaspoon minced garlic   5 ml
½ teaspoon dried thyme leaves   2 ml
10 - 12 small new (red) potatoes with skins
1 (10 ounce) can chicken broth   280 g
1 cup burgundy wine   250 ml
6 bacon slices, cooked, crumbled

- Brown chicken quarters in oil on both sides in skillet and set aside.

- Place onions, mushrooms, garlic and thyme in sprayed oval
  slow cooker.

- Add chicken quarters, potatoes, chicken broth and a little salt and
  pepper.

- Cover and cook on LOW for 8 to 10 hours or on HIGH for 3 to 4 hours.

- During last hour, turn heat to HIGH, add wine and continue cooking.

- Sprinkle crumbled bacon over chicken before serving. Serves 4 to 6.

Mexican Chicken

3 cups cooked, chopped chicken	420 g
1 (1 ounce) packet taco seasoning	30 g
1 cup rice	185 g
2 cups chopped celery	200 g
1 green bell pepper, seeded, chopped	
2 (15 ounce) cans Mexican stewed tomatoes	2 (425 g)

- Combine chicken, taco seasoning, rice, celery, bell pepper and stewed tomatoes in bowl and mix well.

- Pour into sprayed 5-quart (5 L) slow cooker. Cover and cook on LOW for 4 to 5 hours. Serves 4 to 6.

Simple Chicken Tropic

1 (2½ - 3 pound) chicken, quartered	1.1 - 1.4 kg
1 teaspoon dried oregano	5 ml
2 teaspoons minced garlic	10 ml
2 tablespoons butter	30 g
¼ cup lemon juice	60 ml

- Season chicken quarters with a little salt, pepper and oregano and rub garlic on chicken. Brown chicken quarters on all sides in butter in skillet and transfer to sprayed, oval slow cooker.

- Add ⅓ cup (75 ml) water to skillet, scrape bottom and pour over chicken.

- Cover and cook on LOW for 5 to 6 hours.

- Pour lemon juice over chicken and continue cooking on LOW for additional 1 hour. Serves 4 to 6.

Saffron-Rice Chicken

1 fryer-broiler chicken, quartered	
½ teaspoon garlic powder	2 ml
Canola oil	
1 (14 ounce) can chicken broth	395 g
1 onion, chopped	
1 green bell pepper, seeded, quartered	
1 yellow bell pepper, seeded, quartered	
1 (4 ounce) jar pimentos, drained	115 g
⅓ cup bacon bits	35 g
1 (5 ounce) package saffron yellow rice mix	145 g
2 tablespoons butter, melted	30 g

- Sprinkle chicken with garlic powder and a little salt and pepper.

- Brown chicken quarters in a little oil in skillet.

- Place chicken in sprayed, oval slow cooker and pour broth over it.

- Combine onion, bell peppers, pimentos and bacon bits in bowl and spoon over chicken quarters.

- Cover and cook on LOW for 4 to 5 hours.

- Carefully remove chicken quarters from cooker, stir in rice mix and butter and return chicken to cooker.

- Cover and cook for 1 hour or until rice is tender. Serves 4 to 6.

Roast Chicken with Veggies

1 (2½ - 3 pound) whole chicken, quartered	1.1 - 1.4 kg
1 (16 ounce) package baby carrots	455 g
4 potatoes, peeled, sliced	
3 ribs celery, sliced	
1 onion, peeled, sliced	
1 cup Italian salad dressing	250 ml
⅔ cup chicken broth	150 ml

- Rinse and dry chicken quarters. Place in sprayed 6-quart (6 L) slow cooker with carrots, potatoes, celery and onion.

- Pour salad dressing and chicken broth over chicken and vegetables.

- Cover and cook on LOW for 6 to 8 hours. Serves 4 to 6.

Slow Cooker "Baked" Chicken

1 cup rice	185 g
2 (10 ounce) cans cream of chicken soup	2 (280 g)
1 (14 ounce) can chicken broth	395 g
1 (1 ounce) packet dry onion soup mix	30 g
1 chicken, quartered	

- Place rice in sprayed 5 to 6-quart (5 to 6 L) oval slow cooker.

- Combine soup, broth, 2 soup cans water and onion soup mix in saucepan and mix well. Heat just enough to mix ingredients.

- Spoon half soup mixture over rice and place chicken quarters in slow cooker. Spoon remaining soup mixture over chicken.

- Cover and cook on LOW for 5 to 6 hours. Serves 4 to 6.

Caribbean Chicken Special

1 whole chicken, quartered	
½ cup plus 2 tablespoons flour, divided	75 g
½ teaspoon ground nutmeg	2 ml
½ teaspoon ground cinnamon	2 ml
2 large sweet potatoes, peeled, sliced	
1 (8 ounce) can pineapple chunks with juice	230 g
1 (10 ounce) can cream of chicken soup	280 g
⅔ cup orange juice	150 ml
Rice, cooked	
Butter	

- Wash chicken quarters and dry with paper towels.

- Combine ½ cup (60 g) flour, nutmeg and cinnamon in bowl.

- Coat chicken with flour mixture.

- Place sweet potatoes and pineapple in large, sprayed slow cooker. Arrange chicken on top.

- Combine soup, orange juice and remaining flour in bowl and pour over chicken.

- Cover and cook on LOW for 7 to 9 hours or on HIGH for 3 to 4 hours. Serve over buttered rice. Serves 4 to 6.

Chicken, Honey

2 small fryer chickens, quartered	
½ cup (1 stick) butter, melted	**115 g**
⅔ cup honey	**225 g**
¼ cup dijon-style mustard	**60 g**
1 teaspoon curry powder	**5 ml**

- Place chicken pieces in large, sprayed slow cooker, skin-side up and sprinkle a little salt over chicken.

- Combine butter, honey, mustard and curry powder in bowl and mix well.

- Pour butter-mustard mixture over chicken quarters.

- Cover and cook on LOW for 6 to 8 hours. Baste chicken once during cooking. Serves 6 to 8.

57 Sauce Chicken

1 large fryer chicken, quartered	
2 tablespoons butter	**30 g**
½ cup Heinz® 57 Sauce	**135 g**
1 (15 ounce) can stewed tomatoes	**425 g**

- Place chicken in sprayed, large slow cooker.

- Combine butter, 57 Sauce and stewed tomatoes in saucepan. Heat just until butter melts and ingredients mix well. Pour over chicken.

- Cover and cook on LOW for 5 to 6 hours. Serves 4 to 6.

Chicken 1-Dish Meal

4 boneless, skinless chicken breast halves
2 (10 ounce) jars sweet-and-sour sauce   2 (280 g)
1 (16 ounce) package frozen broccoli, cauliflower
    and carrots, thawed   455 g
1 (10 ounce) package frozen baby peas, thawed   280 g
2 cups sliced celery   200 g
1 (6 ounce) package parmesan-butter rice mix   170 g
⅓ cup toasted, slivered almonds   55 g

- Cut chicken in 1-inch (2.5 cm) strips.

- Combine chicken pieces, sweet-and-sour sauce and all vegetables in sprayed 6-quart (6 L) slow cooker.

- Cover and cook on LOW for 4 to 6 hours.

- When ready to serve, cook parmesan-butter rice according to package directions and fold in almonds.

- Serve chicken and vegetables over rice. Serves 4.

Keep all foods that need refrigeration cold and in the refrigerator before cooking in the slow cooker. It takes several hours for the cooker to reach bacteria-killing temperatures so keep all foods cold before they go in. If possible, you can start the slow cooker on HIGH for about 1 hour and reduce the heat to LOW for the longer cooking times.

Celebration Chicken

4 large boneless, skinless chicken breast halves
Chicken seasoning
4 slices American cheese
1 (10 ounce) can cream of celery soup   **280 g**
½ cup sour cream   **120 g**
1 (6 ounce) box chicken stuffing mix   **170 g**
½ cup (1 stick) butter, melted   **115 g**

- Place chicken in sprayed, oval slow cooker. Sprinkle each breast with chicken seasoning.

- Place slice of cheese on top.

- Combine celery soup and sour cream in saucepan and heat just enough to mix well and spoon over chicken and cheese.

- Sprinkle chicken stuffing mix over top of cheese. Drizzle melted butter over stuffing mix.

- Cover and cook on LOW for 5 to 6 hours. Serves 4.

Southwestern Slow Cook

6 boneless, skinless chicken breast halves	
1 teaspoon ground cumin	**5 ml**
1 teaspoon chili powder	**5 ml**
1 (10 ounce) can cream of chicken soup	**280 g**
1 (10 ounce) can fiesta nacho cheese soup	**280 g**
1 cup salsa	**265 g**
Rice, cooked	
Flour tortillas	

- Sprinkle chicken breasts with cumin, chili powder and a little salt and pepper and place in sprayed, oval slow cooker.

- Combine soups and salsa in saucepan. Heat just enough to mix and pour over chicken breasts.

- Cover and cook on LOW for 6 to 7 hours. Serve over rice with warmed flour tortillas spread with butter. Serves 6.

Orange Chicken

6 boneless, skinless chicken breast halves	
Canola oil	
1 (1 ounce) packet onion soup mix	**30 g**
1 (6 ounce) can frozen orange juice concentrate, thawed	**175 ml**

- Brown chicken breasts in little oil in skillet and place in sprayed, large slow cooker.

- Combine onion soup mix, orange juice concentrate and ½ cup (125 ml) water in bowl and pour over chicken.

- Cover and cook on LOW for 3 to 5 hours. Serves 6.

Mozzarella Chicken Breasts

4 boneless, skinless chicken breast halves	
1 (10 ounce) can French onion soup	280 g
2 teaspoons chicken seasoning	10 ml
1 (4 ounce) jar sliced mushrooms, drained	115 g
1 cup shredded mozzarella cheese	115 g
Green onions, chopped	

- Brown chicken breasts in skillet and place in sprayed, oval slow cooker.

- Pour soup over chicken and sprinkle a little pepper and chicken seasoning over chicken breasts.

- Place mushrooms and cheese on top.

- Cover and cook on LOW for 4 to 5 hours. When ready to serve, sprinkle some chopped green onions over each serving. Serves 4.

Chick Delicious

There is a lot of delicious sauce.

5 - 6 boneless, skinless chicken breast halves	
1 teaspoon chicken seasoning	**5 ml**
1 (10 ounce) can cream of chicken soup	**280 g**
1 (10 ounce) can broccoli-cheese soup	**280 g**
½ cup white wine	**125 ml**
Noodles, cooked	

- Place chicken, sprinkled with a little pepper and chicken seasoning, in sprayed, oval slow cooker.

- Combine soups and wine in saucepan and heat enough to mix well. Pour over chicken.

- Cover and cook on LOW for 5 to 6 hours.

- Serve chicken and sauce over noodles. Serves 5 to 6.

TIP: This is great served with oven-baked roasted garlic Italian toast.

TIP: If chicken breasts are very large, cut in half lengthwise.

Chicken with Spinach Fettuccini

2 pounds boneless, skinless chicken thighs, cubed	910 g
½ teaspoon garlic powder	2 ml
1 red bell pepper, seeded, chopped	
2 ribs celery, chopped	
1 (10 ounce) can cream of celery soup	280 g
1 (10 ounce) can cream of chicken soup	280 g
1 (8 ounce) package cubed Velveeta® cheese	230 g
1 (4 ounce) jar diced pimentos	115 g
1 (16 ounce) package spinach fettuccini	455 g

- Place chicken in sprayed slow cooker. Sprinkle with garlic powder, ½ teaspoon (2 ml) pepper, bell pepper and celery. Top with soups.

- Cover and cook on HIGH for 4 to 6 hours or until chicken juices are clear.

- Stir in cheese and pimentos. Cover and cook until cheese melts.

- Cook fettuccini according to package directions and drain.

- Place fettuccini in serving bowl and spoon chicken over fettuccini. Serve hot. Serves 4 to 6.

Hearty Chicken Pot

1 pound chicken tenderloins	455 g
Canola oil	
1 pound Polish sausage, cut in 1-inch (2.5 cm) pieces	455 g
2 onions, chopped	
1 (31 ounce) can pork and beans with liquid	880 g
1 (15 ounce) can Ranch Style® or chili beans, drained	425 g
1 (15 ounce) can great northern beans	425 g
1 (15 ounce) can butter beans, drained	425 g
1 cup ketchup	270 g
1 cup packed brown sugar	220 g
1 tablespoon vinegar	15 ml
6 slices bacon, cooked, crumbled	

- Brown chicken slices in a little oil in skillet and place in sprayed, large slow cooker.

- Add sausage, onions, all beans, ketchup, brown sugar and vinegar and stir gently.

- Cover and cook on LOW for 7 to 8 hours or on HIGH for 3 hours 30 minutes to 4 hours.

- When ready to serve, sprinkle crumbled bacon over top. Serves 4 to 6.

Russian-Style Chicken

1 (8 ounce) bottle Russian salad dressing	250 ml
1 (16 ounce) can whole cranberry sauce	455 g
1 (1 ounce) packet dry onion soup mix	30 g
4 skinless chicken quarters*	
Rice, cooked	

- Combine salad dressing, cranberry sauce, ½ cup (125 ml) water and soup mix in bowl. Stir well to get all lumps out of soup mix.

- Place chicken quarters in sprayed 6-quart (6 L) oval slow cooker and spoon dressing-cranberry sauce mixture over chicken.

- Cover and cook on LOW for 4 to 5 hours. Serve sauce and chicken over rice. Serves 4 to 6.

TIP: Use 6 chicken breasts if you don't want to cut up a chicken).

So-Good Chicken

4 - 5 boneless, skinless chicken breast halves	
1 (10 ounce) can golden mushroom soup	280 g
1 cup white cooking wine	250 ml
1 (8 ounce) carton sour cream	230 g

- Place chicken in sprayed slow cooker and sprinkle with a little salt and pepper.

- Whisk mushroom soup, wine and sour cream in bowl and mix well. Spoon over chicken breasts.

- Cover and cook on LOW for 5 to 7 hours. Serves 4 to 5.

Chicken Perfecto

When cooked, you will have a great "gravy"
that is wonderful served over noodles or rice.

1 (2.5 ounce) jar dried beef	**70 g**
6 small boneless, skinless chicken breast halves	
6 slices bacon	
2 (10 ounce) cans golden mushroom soup	**2 (280 g)**

- Line bottom sprayed, oval slow cooker with slices of dried beef and overlap some.

- Wrap each chicken breast with slice of bacon and secure with toothpick. Place in slow cooker, overlapping as little as possible.

- Combine soup and ½ cup (125 ml) water or milk and spoon over chicken breasts.

- Cover and cook on LOW for 6 to 8 hours. Serves 6.

Chicken Season

4 boneless, skinless chicken breast halves	
1 green bell pepper, seeded, cut in rings	
1 (16 ounce) jar picante sauce	**455 g**
⅓ cup packed brown sugar	**75 g**
1 tablespoon mustard	**15 ml**

- Place chicken breasts in sprayed slow cooker with bell pepper rings over top of chicken.

- Combine picante, brown sugar and mustard in bowl and spoon over top of chicken.

- Cover and cook on LOW for 4 to 5 hours. Serves 4.

Chicken Oregano

½ cup (1 stick) butter, melted	**115 g**
1 (1 ounce) packet Italian dressing mix	**30 g**
1 tablespoon lemon juice	**15 ml**
4 - 5 boneless, skinless chicken breast halves	
2 tablespoons dried oregano	**30 ml**

- Combine butter, dressing mix and lemon juice in bowl and mix well.

- Place chicken breasts in sprayed, large slow cooker. Spoon butter-lemon juice mixture over chicken.

- Cover and cook on LOW for 5 to 6 hours.

- One hour before serving, baste chicken with pan juices and sprinkle oregano over chicken. Serves 4 to 5.

Chicken in a Soup

4 - 6 boneless, skinless chicken breast halves
1 (8 ounce) carton sour cream   230 g
¼ cup soy sauce   60 ml
2 (10 ounce) cans French onion soup   2 (280 g)

- Place chicken in sprayed, large slow cooker. Combine sour cream, soy
  sauce and onion soup in bowl, stir and mix well. Pour over chicken.

- Cover and cook on LOW for 5 to 6 hours if chicken breasts are large,
  3 to 4 hours if breasts are medium. Serves 4 to 6.

TIP: Serve chicken and sauce with hot, buttered rice or mashed potatoes.

Mushroom Chicken

4 boneless, skinless chicken breasts halves
1 (15 ounce) can tomato sauce   425 g
2 (4 ounce) cans sliced mushrooms, drained   2 (115 g)
1 (10 ounce) package frozen seasoning blend (onions
     and peppers)   280 g
2 teaspoons Italian seasoning   10 ml
1 teaspoon minced garlic   5 ml

- Brown chicken breasts in skillet and place in sprayed, oval slow cooker.

- Combine tomato sauce, mushrooms, onions and peppers, Italian
  seasoning, minced garlic, and ¼ cup (60 ml) water in bowl and spoon
  over chicken breasts.

- Cover and cook on LOW for 4 to 5 hours. Serves 4.

Russian-Dressed Chicken

6 boneless, skinless chicken breast halves
1 (12 ounce) jar orange marmalade   **340 g**
1 (8 ounce) bottle Russian dressing   **250 ml**
1 (1 ounce) packet onion soup mix   **30 g**

- Place chicken breasts in sprayed, oval slow cooker.

- Combine orange marmalade, dressing, soup mix and ¾ cup (175 ml) water in bowl and stir well. Spoon mixture over chicken breasts.

- Cover and cook on LOW for 4 to 6 hours. Serves 6.

Easy Chicken and Stuffing

5 boneless, skinless chicken breast halves
2 (10 ounce) cans cream of chicken soup   **2 (280 g)**
1 (6 ounce) box chicken stuffing mix   **170 g**
1 (16 ounce) package frozen green peas, thawed, drained   **455 g**

- Place chicken breasts in sprayed 6-quart (6 L) slow cooker and spoon soup over chicken.

- Combine stuffing mix with ingredients on package directions in bowl and spoon over chicken and soup.

- Cover and cook on LOW for 5 to 6 hours.

- Sprinkle green peas over top of stuffing. Cover and cook for additional 45 to 50 minutes. Serves 5.

TIP: Use 1 (10 ounce/280 g) can cream of chicken soup and 1 (10 ounce/280 g) can fiesta nacho soup for a nice variation.

Wild Chicken Crunch

1 (6 ounce) box long grain-wild rice mix	**170 g**
1 (16 ounce) jar roasted garlic parmesan cheese creation	**455 g**
6 boneless, skinless chicken breast halves	
1 (16 ounce) box frozen French-style green beans, thawed	**455 g**
½ cup slivered almonds, toasted	**85 g**

- Pour 2½ cups (625 ml) water, rice and seasoning packet in sprayed, oval slow cooker and stir well.

- Spoon in cheese creation and mix well. Place chicken breasts in slow cooker and cover with green beans.

- Cover and cook on LOW for 3 to 5 hours. When ready to serve, sprinkle with slivered almonds. Serves 6.

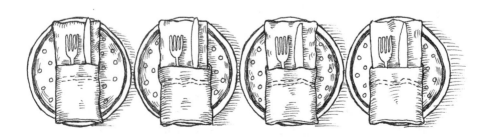

Dinner in a Dish

5 boneless, skinless chicken breast halves	
6 medium new (red) potatoes with peel, cubed	
6 medium carrots, chopped	
1 tablespoon dried parsley flakes	**15 ml**
1 teaspoon seasoned salt	**5 ml**
1 (10 ounce) can golden mushroom soup	**280 g**
1 (10 ounce) can cream of chicken soup	**280 g**
¼ cup dried mashed potato flakes	**15 g**
Water or milk	

- Cut chicken into ½-inch (1.2 cm) pieces.

- Place potatoes and carrots in sprayed slow cooker and top with chicken breasts.

- Sprinkle parsley flakes, seasoned salt and ½ teaspoon (2 ml) pepper over chicken. Combine soups in bowl and spread over chicken.

- Cover and cook on LOW for 6 to 7 hours.

- Stir in potato flakes and a little water or milk if necessary to make gravy and cook for additional 30 minutes. Serves 5.

Cheese-Blend Chicken Dinner

1 (8 ounce) package medium egg noodles	230 g
4 - 5 boneless, skinless chicken breast halves	
1 (14 ounce) can chicken broth	395 g
2 cups sliced celery	200 g
2 onions, chopped	
1 green bell pepper, seeded, chopped	
1 red bell pepper, seeded, chopped	
1 (10 ounce) can cream of chicken soup	280 g
1 (10 ounce) can cream of mushroom soup	280 g
1 cup shredded 4-cheese blend	115 g

- Cook noodles in boiling water until barely tender and drain well.

- Cut chicken into thin slices.

- Combine noodles, chicken and chicken broth in sprayed, large slow cooker and mix. Make sure noodles separate and coat with broth.

- Stir in remaining ingredients.

- Cover and cook on LOW for 4 to 6 hours. Serves 4 to 5.

Angel Chicken

1 pound chicken tenders	455 g
Lemon-herb chicken seasoning	
3 tablespoons butter	45 g
1 onion, coarsely chopped	
1 (15 ounce) can diced tomatoes	425 g
1 (10 ounce) can golden mushroom soup	280 g
1 (8 ounce) box angel hair pasta	230 g

- Pat chicken tenders dry with several paper towels and sprinkle with ample amount of chicken seasoning.

- Melt butter in large skillet, brown chicken and place in sprayed, oval slow cooker. Pour remaining butter from skillet over chicken and cover with onion.

- Combine tomatoes and mushroom soup in bowl and pour over chicken and onions.

- Cover and cook on LOW for 4 to 5 hours.

- When ready to serve, cook pasta according to package directions. Serve chicken and sauce over pasta. Serves 4.

Cordon Bleu Special

4 boneless, skinless chicken breast halves
4 slices cooked ham
4 slices Swiss cheese
1 (10 ounce) can cream of chicken soup   **280 g**
¼ cup milk   **60 ml**
Noodles, cooked

- Place chicken breasts on cutting board and pound until breast halves are thin.

- Place ham and cheese slices on chicken breasts, roll and secure with toothpick.

- Arrange chicken rolls in sprayed 4-quart (4 L) slow cooker.

- Combine chicken soup and milk in saucepan, heat just enough to mix well and pour over chicken rolls.

- Cover and cook on LOW for 4 to 5 hours.

- Serve over noodles. Serves 4.

Tasty Salsa Chicken

4 - 5 boneless, skinless chicken breast halves	
1 (1 ounce) packet taco seasoning mix	30 g
1 cup salsa	265 g
½ cup sour cream	120 g

- Place chicken breasts in sprayed 5 to 6-quart (5 to 6 L) slow cooker and add ¼ cup (60 ml) water. Sprinkle taco seasoning mix over chicken and top with salsa.

- Cook on LOW for 5 to 6 hours.

- When ready to serve, remove chicken breasts and place on platter. Stir sour cream into salsa sauce and spoon over chicken breasts. Serves 4 to 5.

Alfredo Chicken Blend

4 - 5 boneless, skinless chicken breast halves	
1 (15 ounce) can whole kernel corn, drained	425 g
1 (10 ounce) package frozen green peas, thawed	280 g
1 (16 ounce) jar alfredo sauce	455 g
1 teaspoon chicken seasoning	5 ml
1 teaspoon minced garlic	5 ml
Pasta, cooked	

- Brown chicken breasts in skillet and place in sprayed, oval slow cooker.

- Combine corn, peas, alfredo sauce, ¼ cup (60 ml) water, seasoning and minced garlic in bowl and spoon mixture over chicken breasts.

- Cover and cook on LOW for 4 to 5 hours. Serve over pasta. Serves 4 to 5.

Chicken and Creamed Vegetables

4 large boneless, skinless chicken breast halves
1 (10 ounce) can cream of chicken soup   **280 g**
1 (16 ounce) package frozen peas and carrots, thawed   **455 g**
1 (12 ounce) jar chicken gravy   **340 g**
Biscuits or Texas toast

- Cut chicken in thin slices.

- Pour soup and ½ cup (125 ml) water into sprayed 6-quart (6 L) slow cooker, mix and add chicken slices.

- Sprinkle a little salt and lots of pepper over chicken and soup.

- Cover and cook on LOW for 4 to 5 hours.

- Add peas and carrots, chicken gravy and ½ cup (125 ml) water. Increase heat to HIGH and cook for about 1 hour or until peas and carrots are tender.

- Serve over biscuits or Texas toast (thick slices of bread). Serves 4.

Slow cookers aren't just for cooking when it's cold and wintry outside. These are also great to use in the summer so you don't heat up the kitchen with the oven.

Bell Peppered Chicken

4 large boneless, skinless chicken breast halves
Lemon juice
1 red bell pepper, seeded, chopped
2 ribs celery, sliced diagonally
1 (10 ounce) can cream of chicken soup 280 g
1 (10 ounce) can cream of celery soup 280 g
⅓ cup dry white wine 75 ml
1 (4 ounce) package shredded parmesan cheese 115 g
Rice, cooked

- Wash chicken and pat dry with paper towels, rub a little lemon juice over chicken and sprinkle with a little salt and pepper.

- Place in sprayed slow cooker and top with bell pepper and celery.

- Combine soups and wine in saucepan and heat just enough to mix thoroughly.

- Pour over chicken breasts and sprinkle with parmesan cheese.

- Cover and cook on LOW for 6 to 7 hours. Serve over rice. Serves 4.

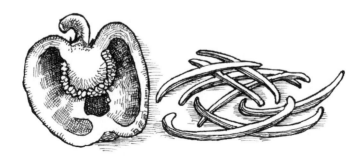

Garlic-Flavored Chicken Dinner

1 (6 ounce) box long grain-wild rice mix	170 g
1 (16 ounce) jar roasted garlic parmesan cheese creation	455 g
12 - 15 frozen chicken breast tenderloins, thawed	
1 cup frozen petite green peas, thawed	145 g

- Pour 2½ cups (625 ml) water, rice and seasoning packet into sprayed 5-quart (5 L) slow cooker and stir well. Add cheese creation and mix well.

- Place chicken tenderloins in slow cooker and cover with green peas.

- Cover and cook on LOW for 4 to 5 hours. Serves 4.

New Potato Chicken

4 boneless, skinless chicken breast halves	
2 teaspoons chicken seasoning	10 ml
8 - 10 small new (red) potatoes with peel	
1 (10 ounce) can cream of chicken soup	280 g
1 (8 ounce) carton sour cream	230 g

- Place chicken breast halves in sprayed slow cooker and sprinkle with chicken seasoning.

- Arrange potatoes around chicken.

- Combine soup, sour cream and good amount of pepper in bowl. Spoon over chicken breasts.

- Cover and cook on LOW for 4 to 6 hours. Serves 4.

Bamboo Chicken

4 boneless, skinless chicken breast halves	
2 - 3 cups sliced celery	200 - 300 g
1 onion, coarsely chopped	
⅓ cup soy sauce	75 ml
¼ teaspoon cayenne pepper	1 ml
1 (14 ounce) can chicken broth	395 g
1 (16 ounce) can bean sprouts, drained	455 g
1 (8 ounce) can sliced water chestnuts, drained	230 g
1 (6 ounce) can bamboo shoots	170 g
¼ cup flour	30 g
Chow mein noodles	

- Combine chicken, celery, onion, soy sauce, cayenne pepper and chicken broth in sprayed slow cooker.

- Cover and cook on LOW for 3 to 4 hours.

- Add bean sprouts, water chestnuts and bamboo shoots. Mix flour and ¼ cup (60 ml) water in bowl and stir into chicken and vegetables. Cook for additional 1 hour.

- Serve over chow mein noodles. Serves 4.

Chicken and Potatoes

6 medium new (red) potatoes with peels, quartered	
4 - 5 carrots, quartered	
4 - 5 boneless, skinless chicken breast halves	
1 tablespoon chicken seasoning	**15 ml**
2 (10 ounce) cans cream of chicken soup	**2 (280 g)**
⅓ cup white wine or cooking wine	**75 ml**

- Cut carrots into ½-inch (1.2 cm) pieces. Place potatoes and carrots in sprayed slow cooker.

- Sprinkle chicken breasts with chicken seasoning and place over vegetables.

- Heat soup and ¼ cup (60 ml) water in saucepan just to mix and pour over chicken and vegetables.

- Cover and cook on LOW for 5 to 6 hours. Serves 4 to 5.

TIP: Instead of cream of chicken soup, try 1 (10 ounce/280 g) can chicken soup and 1 (10 ounce/280 g) can mushroom soup for a tasty change.

Cook-and-Serve Chicken

5 boneless, skinless chicken breast halves
1 (16 ounce) jar alfredo sauce 455 g
1 (16 ounce) package frozen green peas, thawed 455 g
1½ cups shredded mozzarella cheese 175 g
Noodles, cooked

- Cut chicken into strips and place in sprayed slow cooker.

- Combine alfredo sauce, peas and cheese in bowl and mix well. Spoon over chicken strips.

- Cover and cook on LOW for 5 to 6 hours.

- When ready to serve, spoon over noodles. Serves 5.

Simple Chicken Supper

1 (6 ounce) package stuffing mix 170 g
3 cups cooked, chopped chicken breasts 420 g
1 (16 ounce) package frozen whole green beans, thawed 455 g
2 (12 ounce) jars chicken gravy 2 (340 g)

- Prepare stuffing mix according to package directions and place in sprayed, oval slow cooker.

- Follow with layer of chicken and place green beans over chicken. Pour chicken gravy over green beans.

- Cover and cook on LOW for 3 hours 30 minutes to 4 hours. Serves 4 to 6.

Wine-and-Dine Chicken

4 slices bacon
5 - 6 boneless, skinless chicken breast halves
1 cup sliced celery   200 g
1 cup sliced red bell pepper   90 g
1 (10 ounce) can cream of chicken soup   280 g
2 tablespoons white wine or cooking wine   30 ml
6 slices Swiss cheese
2 tablespoons dried parsley   30 ml

- Cook bacon in large skillet, drain, crumble and reserve drippings.

- Place chicken in skillet with bacon drippings and lightly brown on both sides.

- Transfer chicken to sprayed, oval slow cooker and place celery and bell pepper over chicken.

- In same skillet, combine soup and wine, stir and spoon over vegetables and chicken.

- Cover and cook on LOW for 3 to 4 hours. Top with slices of cheese over each chicken breast and cook for additional 10 minutes.

- Serve with its sauce and sprinkle with crumbled bacon. Serves 5 to 6.

Chicken Marseilles

4 - 5 boneless, skinless chicken breast halves	
2 tablespoons butter	**30 g**
1 (2 ounce) packet leek soup and dip mix	**60 g**
½ teaspoon dill weed	**2 ml**
1 cup milk	**250 ml**
Brown rice, cooked	
¾ cup sour cream	**180 g**

- Place chicken breasts in sprayed, large slow cooker.

- Combine butter, leek soup mix, dill weed, milk and ½ cup (125 ml) water in saucepan and heat just enough for butter to melt and ingredients to mix well. Pour over chicken.

- Cover and cook on LOW for 3 to 5 hours.

- When ready to serve, remove chicken breasts to platter with rice and cover to keep warm.

- Add sour cream to liquid in cooker and stir well. Pour sauce over chicken and rice. Serves 4 to 5.

One-Dish Chicken Meal

5 - 6 boneless, skinless chicken breast halves
6 carrots, cut in 1-inch lengths   **2.5 cm**
1 (15 ounce) can cut green beans, drained   **425 g**
1 (15 ounce) can whole new potatoes, drained   **425 g**
2 (10 ounce) cans cream of mushroom soup   **2 (280 g)**
Shredded cheddar cheese

- Wash chicken breasts and dry with paper towels. Place in sprayed, oval slow cooker.

- Combine carrots, green beans, potatoes and mushroom soup in bowl and pour over chicken.

- Cover and cook on LOW for 8 to 10 hours.

- When ready to serve, sprinkle cheese over top. Serves 5 to 6.

Easy Chicken Fajitas

2 pounds boneless, skinless chicken breast halves	910 g
1 onion, thinly sliced	
1 red bell pepper, seeded, julienned	
1 teaspoon ground cumin	5 ml
1½ teaspoons chili powder	7 ml
1 tablespoon lime juice	15 ml
½ cup chicken broth	125 ml
8 - 10 warm flour tortillas	
Guacamole	
Sour cream	
Lettuce	
Diced tomatoes	

- Cut chicken into diagonal strips and place in sprayed slow cooker. Top with onion and bell pepper.

- Combine cumin, chili powder, lime juice and chicken broth in bowl and pour over chicken and vegetables.

- Cover and cook on LOW for 5 to 7 hours.

- When serving, spoon several slices of chicken mixture with sauce into center of each warm tortilla and fold.

- Serve with guacamole, sour cream, lettuce, and/or tomatoes. Serves 4 to 6.

Pimento Chicken

1 cup rice	185 g
1 tablespoon chicken seasoning	15 ml
1 (1 ounce) packet onion soup mix	30 g
1 green bell pepper, seeded, chopped	
1 (4 ounce) jar diced pimentos, drained	115 g
¾ teaspoon dried basil	4 ml
1 (14 ounce) can chicken broth	395 g
1 (10 ounce) can cream of chicken soup	280 g
5 - 6 boneless, skinless chicken breast halves	

- Combine rice, chicken seasoning, onion soup mix, bell pepper, pimentos, basil, broth, ½ cup (125 ml) water and chicken soup in bowl and mix well.

- Place chicken breasts in sprayed, oval slow cooker and cover with rice mixture.

- Cover and cook on LOW for 6 to 7 hours. Serves 5 to 6.

When you want to adapt a recipe for the slow cooker,
it is best to reduce the liquid unless rice or pasta is used.
Slow cooking retains the moisture already in the ingredients
unlike stovetop cooking or baking in the oven. If rice or
pasta is used, 1 cup (250 ml) liquid will usually work well.

Celery-Rice Chicken

¾ cup rice	140 g
1 (14 ounce) can chicken broth	395 g
1 (1 ounce) packet dry onion soup mix	30 g
1 red bell pepper, seeded, chopped	
2 (10 ounce) cans cream of celery soup	2 (280 g)
¾ cup white cooking wine	175 ml
4 - 6 boneless skinless chicken breast halves	
1 (3 ounce) package fresh parmesan cheese	85 g

- Combine rice, broth, soup mix, bell pepper, celery soup, ¾ cup (175 ml) water, wine and several sprinkles of pepper in bowl and mix well. (Make sure to mix soup well with liquids.)

- Place chicken breasts in sprayed 6-quart (6 L) slow cooker.

- Pour rice-soup mixture over chicken breasts.

- Cover and cook on LOW for 4 to 6 hours.

- One hour before serving, sprinkle parmesan cheese over chicken. Serves 4 to 6.

Easy Delicious Chicken

5 - 6 boneless skinless chicken breast halves	
2 tablespoons butter	30 g
1 (16 ounce) package frozen broccoli florets, thawed	455 g
1 red bell pepper, seeded, julienned	
1 (16 ounce) jar parmesan-mozzarella cheese creations sauce	455 g
3 tablespoons sherry	45 ml
Noodles, cooked	

- Brown chicken breasts in butter in skillet and place in sprayed 5 to 6-quart (5 to 6 L) oval slow cooker.

- Remove and discard stems from broccoli florets.

- Combine broccoli florets, bell pepper, cheese sauce and sherry in bowl and mix well. Spoon over chicken breasts.

- Cover and cook on LOW for 4 to 5 hours. Serve over noodles. Serves 5 to 6.

Curried Chicken

3 large boneless, skinless chicken breast halves
½ cup chicken broth   125 ml
1 (10 ounce) can cream of chicken soup   230 g
1 onion, coarsely chopped
1 red bell pepper, seeded, julienned
¼ cup golden raisins   40 g
1½ teaspoons curry powder   7 ml
¼ teaspoon ground ginger   1 ml
Rice, cooked

- Cut chicken breasts into thin strips and place in sprayed 5 to 6-quart (5 to 6 L) slow cooker.

- Combine broth, soup, onion, bell pepper, raisins, curry powder and ginger in bowl and mix well. Pour over chicken.

- Cover and cook on LOW for 3 to 4 hours. Serve over rice. Serves 4.

It is best to check your seasonings after cooking. Over long periods of time the flavors may cook out and you may need to add some seasonings again. You can, in fact, reduce sodium intake by waiting to add salt until after the dish has been cooked.

Vegetable-Chicken Mix

4 - 5 boneless, skinless chicken breast halves
2 teaspoons seasoned salt   **10 ml**
1 (16 ounce) package frozen broccoli, cauliflower
   and carrots, thawed   **455 g**
1 (10 ounce) can cream of celery soup   **280 g**
1 (8 ounce) package shredded cheddar-Jack cheese, divided   **230 g**

- Cut chicken into strips, sprinkle with seasoned salt and place in sprayed slow cooker.

- Combine vegetables, soup and half cheese and mix well. Spoon over chicken breasts.

- Cover and cook on LOW for 4 to 5 hours.

- About 10 minutes before serving, sprinkle remaining cheese on top. Serves 4 to 5.

Italian-Seasoned Chicken

1 (16 ounce) package frozen whole green beans, thawed	455 g
1 onion, chopped	
1 cup fresh mushroom halves	70 g
3 boneless, skinless chicken breast halves	
1 (15 ounce) can Italian stewed tomatoes	425 g
1 teaspoon chicken bouillon granules	5 ml
1 teaspoon minced garlic	5 ml
1 teaspoon Italian seasoning	5 ml
1 (8 ounce) package fettuccine	230 g
1 (4 ounce) package grated parmesan cheese	115 g

- Place green beans, onion and mushrooms in sprayed 4-quart (4 L) slow cooker.

- Cut chicken into 1-inch (2.5 cm) pieces and place over vegetables.

- Combine stewed tomatoes, chicken bouillon, garlic and Italian seasoning in bowl. Pour over chicken.

- Cover and cook on LOW for 5 to 6 hours.

- Cook fettuccine according to package directions and drain.

- Serve chicken over fettuccini and sprinkle with parmesan cheese. Serves 4.

TIP: Add ¼ cup (60 g) butter to give this dish a richer taste.

Chinese Chicken and Noodles

2 pounds boneless, skinless chicken breast halves	910 g
¼ cup cornstarch	30 g
⅓ cup soy sauce	75 ml
2 onions, chopped	
3 ribs celery, sliced diagonally	
1 red bell pepper, julienned	
2 (14 ounce) cans mixed Chinese vegetables, drained	2 (395 g)
¼ cup molasses	60 ml
Chow mein noodles	

- Place chicken breasts and 2 cups (500 ml) water in sprayed slow cooker. Cover and cook on LOW for 3 to 4 hours.

- One hour before serving, remove chicken and cut into bite-size pieces.

- Combine cornstarch and soy sauce in bowl and mix well. Stir into liquid in slow cooker.

- Add chicken, onions, celery, bell pepper, mixed vegetables and molasses. Turn heat to HIGH, cover and cook for additional 1 to 2 hours.

- Serve over chow mein noodles. Serves 4 to 6.

Cheesy Broccoli Chicken

4 boneless, skinless chicken breast halves	
2 tablespoons butter, melted	**30 g**
1 (10 ounce) can broccoli-cheese soup	**280 g**
¼ cup milk	**60 ml**
1 (10 ounce) package frozen broccoli spears	**280 g**
Rice, cooked	

- Dry chicken breasts with paper towels and place in sprayed, oval slow cooker. Combine melted butter, soup and milk in bowl and spoon over chicken.

- Cover and cook on LOW for 4 to 6 hours.

- Remove cooker lid and place broccoli over chicken. Cover and cook for additional 1 hour. Serve over rice. Serves 4.

Creamy Chicken Dinner

4 boneless, skinless chicken breast halves	
2 tablespoons butter, melted	**30 g**
1 (10 ounce) can cream of mushroom soup	**280 g**
2 tablespoons dry Italian dressing mix	**30 ml**
½ cup sherry	**125 ml**
1 (8 ounce) package cream cheese, cubed	**230 g**
Noodles, cooked	

- Wash chicken breasts, dry with paper towels and brush melted butter over chicken. Place in sprayed, oval slow cooker and add remaining ingredients except noodles.

- Cover and cook on LOW for 6 to 7 hours. Serve over noodles. Serves 4.

Bacon-Chicken Wraps

1 (2.5 ounce) jar dried beef   70 g
6 boneless, skinless chicken breast halves
6 slices bacon
2 (10 ounce) cans golden mushroom soup   2 (280 g)
1 (6 ounce) package parmesan-butter rice, prepared
   according to package directions   170 g

- Place dried beef sliced in sprayed 5-quart (5 L) slow cooker.

- Roll each chicken breast half in slice of bacon and place over dried beef.

- Heat soup and ⅓ cup (75 ml) water in saucepan just enough to mix well and pour over chicken.

- Cover and cook on LOW for 7 to 8 hours. Serve over rice. Serves 6.

Tuxedo Chicken

1½ pounds boneless, skinless chicken breast tenders	680 g
1 (15 ounce) can artichoke hearts, quartered	425 g
¾ cup chopped, roasted red peppers	195 g
1 (8 ounce) package shredded American cheese	230 g
1 tablespoon marinade for chicken	15 ml
1 (10 ounce) can cream of chicken soup	280 g
1 (8 ounce) package shredded cheddar cheese	230 g
4 cups cooked bow-tie pasta	560 g

- Combine chicken tenders, artichoke hearts, roasted peppers, American cheese, marinade for chicken and soup in sprayed slow cooker and mix well.

- Cover and cook on LOW for 6 to 8 hours.

- About 20 minutes before serving, fold in cheddar cheese, hot pasta and a little salt and pepper. Serves 4.

Once the dish is cooked and served, do not store in cooker so you can avoid development of harmful bacteria. Remove leftovers and refrigerate. Do not heat leftovers in the slow cooker.

Cream of Broccoli Chicken

1¼ cups rice	230 g
2 pounds boneless, skinless chicken breasts	910 g
Dried parsley	
1 (1.8 ounce) packet cream of broccoli soup mix	50 g
1 (14 ounce) can chicken broth	395 g

- Place rice in sprayed slow cooker. Cut chicken into slices and place over rice. Sprinkle with parsley and a little pepper.

- Combine soup mix, chicken broth and 1 cup (250 ml) water in saucepan. Heat just enough to mix well.

- Pour over chicken and rice. Cover and cook on LOW for 6 to 8 hours. Serves 4 to 6.

Special Chicken Fix

1¾ cups flour	210 g
Scant 2 tablespoons dry mustard	30 ml
6 boneless, skinless chicken breast halves	
2 tablespoons canola oil	30 ml
1 (10 ounce) can chicken and rice soup	280 g

- Place flour and mustard in shallow bowl and dredge chicken to coat on all sides. Brown chicken breasts in oil in skillet. Place breasts in sprayed 6-quart (6 L) oval slow cooker.

- Pour soup over chicken and add about ¼ cup (60 ml) water.

- Cover and cook on LOW for 6 to 7 hours. Serves 6.

Apricot-Sauced Chicken

6 boneless, skinless chicken breasts halves
1 (12 ounce) jar apricot preserves   340 g
1 (8 ounce) bottle Catalina dressing   250 ml
1 (1 ounce) packet onion soup mix   30 g

- Place chicken in sprayed 6-quart (6 L) slow cooker.

- Combine apricot preserves, Catalina dressing, onion soup mix, and ¼ cup (60 ml) water in bowl and stir well. Cover chicken breasts with sauce mixture.

- Cover and cook on LOW for 5 to 6 hours. Serves 6.

Southwest Chicken

6 boneless, skinless chicken breast halves
1 (8 ounce) package cream cheese, softened   230 g
1 (16 ounce) jar salsa   455 g
2 teaspoons cumin   10 ml
1 bunch green onions with tops, chopped

- Pound chicken breasts to flatten. Beat cream cheese in bowl until smooth, add salsa, cumin and onions and mix gently.

- Place heaping spoonfuls of cream cheese mixture on each chicken breast and roll. (There will be leftover cream cheese mixture.)

- Place chicken breast seam side-down in sprayed slow cooker. Spoon remaining cream cheese mixture over each chicken roll.

- Cover and cook on LOW for 5 to 6 hours. Serves 6.

Rice-Turkey Night

1 pound turkey sausage	455 g
1 (6 ounce) box flavored rice mix	170 g
2 (14 ounce) cans chicken broth	2 (395 g)
2 cups sliced celery	200 g
1 red bell pepper, seeded, julienned	
1 (15 ounce) can cut green beans, drained	425 g
⅓ cup slivered almonds, toasted	55 g

- Break up turkey sausage and brown in skillet.

- Place in sprayed 4 to 5-quart (4 to 5 L) slow cooker.

- Add rice, 1 cup (250 ml) water, chicken broth, celery, bell pepper and green beans and stir to mix.

- Cover and cook on LOW for 3 to 4 hours.

- When ready to serve, sprinkle almonds over top. Serves 4.

In a large slow cooker, you can make up a big recipe, divide it into batches and freeze for later use. Do not use a slow cooker to reheat leftovers; a microwave oven can quickly bring food to an appropriate temperature.

Turkey Spaghetti

2 pounds ground turkey	**910 g**
2 (10 ounce) cans tomato bisque soup	**2 (280 g)**
1 (14 ounce) can chicken broth	**395 g**
2 (7 ounce) boxes ready-cut spaghetti, cooked, drained	**2 (200 g)**
1 (15 ounce) can whole kernel corn, drained	**425 g**
1 (4 ounce) can sliced mushrooms, drained	**115 g**
¼ cup ketchup	**70 g**

- Cook ground turkey in skillet and season with a little salt and pepper.

- Place turkey in sprayed 5 to 6-quart (5 to 6 L) slow cooker.

- Add soup, broth, spaghetti, corn, mushrooms and ketchup and stir to blend.

- Cover and cook on LOW for 5 to 7 hours or on HIGH for 3 hours. Serves 4 to 6.

Turkey Loaf

2 pounds ground turkey	910 g
1 onion, minced	
½ red bell pepper, seeded, minced	
2 teaspoons minced garlic	10 ml
½ cup chili sauce	135 g
2 large eggs, beaten	
¾ cup Italian seasoned breadcrumbs	90 g

- Make foil handles by cutting 3 (3 x 18 inch/8 x 45 cm) strips of heavy foil; place in bottom of slow cooker in crisscross strips (resembles spokes on wheel) up and over sides.

- Combine all ingredients, 1 teaspoon (5 ml) salt and ½ teaspoon (2 ml) pepper in large bowl and mix well.

- Shape into round loaf and place on foil. Fold extended foil strips over loaf. (When finished cooking, lift loaf out by "handles".)

- Cover and cook on LOW for 5 to 6 hours. Serves 4 to 6.

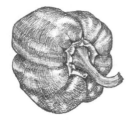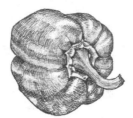

Turkey Surprise

1 (8 ounce) package smoked turkey sausage	230 g
2 cups cooked, cubed turkey	280 g
3 carrots, sliced	
1 onion, halved, sliced	
1 (15 ounce) can navy bean	425 g
1 (15 ounce) can white lima beans	425 g
1 (8 ounce) can tomato sauce	230 g
1 teaspoon dried thyme	5 ml
¼ teaspoon ground allspice	1 ml

- Cut turkey sausage in ½-inch (1.2 cm) pieces.

- Combine all ingredients in sprayed slow cooker.

- Cover and cook on LOW for 4 to 5 hours. Serves 4.

TIP: This is a great recipe for leftover turkey.

Buffalo Legs

12 - 15 chicken legs	
⅓ cup soy sauce	75 ml
⅔ cup packed brown sugar	150 g
⅛ teaspoon ground ginger	.5 ml

- Place chicken legs in sprayed 5-quart (5 L) slow cooker.

- Combine soy sauce, brown sugar, ¼ cup (60 ml) water and ginger in bowl and spoon over chicken legs.

- Cover and cook on LOW for 4 to 5 hours. Serves 6 to 8.

Tasty Turkey Time

1½ pounds turkey tenderloins	680 g
1 (6 ounce) package Oriental rice and vermicelli mix	170 g
1 (10 ounce) package frozen green peas, thawed	280 g
1 cup sliced celery	100 g
¼ cup (½ stick) butter, melted	60 g
1 (14 ounce) can chicken broth	395 g
1½ cups fresh broccoli florets	105 g

- Cut tenderloins into strips.

- Saute turkey strips in non-stick skillet until no longer pink.

- Combine turkey strips, rice-vermicelli mix plus seasoning packet, peas, celery, butter, chicken broth, and 1 cup (250 ml) water in sprayed, large slow cooker and mix well.

- Cover and cook on LOW for 4 to 5 hours.

- Turn heat to HIGH setting, add broccoli and cook for additional 20 minutes. Serves 4 to 6.

Beef
Main Dishes
Ground Beef, Brisket, Roast, Steak

Beef Main Dishes Contents

Potful of Hot Dogs

1 pound beef wieners	455 g
2 (15 ounce) cans chili without beans	2 (425 g)
1 onion, finely chopped	
1 (10 ounce) can cheddar cheese soup	280 g
1 (10 ounce) can fiesta nacho cheese soup	280 g
1 (7 ounce) can chopped green chilies, drained	200 g
Corn chips or tortilla chips	

- Cut wieners in ½-inch (1.2 cm) pieces and place in sprayed slow cooker.

- Combine chili, onion, soups and green chilies in saucepan. (Omit green chilies if serving to kids.)

- Heat just enough to mix ingredients well. Spoon over wieners.

- Cover and cook on LOW for 1 hour 30 minutes to 2 hours

- Serve over bowl of small corn chips or tortilla chips. Serves 4 to 6.

Sloppy Joes

3 pounds ground beef	1.4 kg
1 tablespoon minced garlic	15 ml
1 large onion, finely chopped	
2 ribs celery, chopped	
¼ cup packed brown sugar	55 g
3½ tablespoons mustard	55 g
1 tablespoon chili powder	15 ml
1½ cups ketchup	410 g
3 tablespoons Worcestershire sauce	45 ml

- Brown beef, garlic and onion in very large skillet and drain.

- Combine celery, brown sugar, mustard, chili powder, ketchup and Worcestershire in sprayed 5-quart (5 L) slow cooker. Stir in meat mixture.

- Cover and cook on LOW heat for 6 to 7 hours. Serves 6 to 8.

TIP: This will make enough to fill 16 to 18 hamburger buns.

Italian Tortellini

½ pound ground round steak	230 g
1 (1 pound) package bulk Italian sausage	455 g
1 (15 ounce) carton refrigerated marinara sauce	425 g
1 (15 ounce) can Italian stewed tomatoes	425 g
1½ cups sliced fresh mushrooms	110 g
1 (9 ounce) package refrigerated cheese tortellini	255 g
1½ cups shredded mozzarella cheese	175 g

- Brown and cook ground beef and sausage in large skillet for about 10 minutes on medium-low heat and drain.

- Combine meat mixture, marinara sauce, tomatoes and mushrooms in sprayed 4 to 5-quart (4 to 5 L) slow cooker.

- Cover and cook on LOW 6 to 8 hours.

- Stir in tortellini and sprinkle with mozzarella cheese.

- Turn cooker to HIGH and continue cooking for additional 10 to 15 minutes or until tortellini is tender. Serves 4 to 6.

Beef and Bean Medley

1 pound lean ground beef	455 g
1 onion, chopped	
6 slices bacon, cooked, crumbled	
2 (15 ounce) cans pork and beans	2 (425 g)
1 (15 ounce) can butter beans, rinsed, drained	425 g
1 (15 ounce) can kidney beans, rinsed, drained	425 g
¼ cup ketchup	70 g
½ cup packed brown sugar	110 g
3 tablespoons vinegar	45 ml
1 (13 ounce) bag original corn chips	370 g
1 (8 ounce) package shredded cheddar cheese	230 g

- Brown ground beef and onion in skillet, drain and transfer to sprayed 4 to 5-quart (4 to 5 L) slow cooker.

- Add bacon and all beans.

- Combine ketchup, brown sugar and vinegar in bowl. Add to cooker and stir.

- Cover and cook on LOW for 4 to 6 hours.

- When ready to serve, spoon over corn chips and sprinkle cheese over top. Serves 4 to 6.

Beef and Macaroni Twist

1 (10 ounce) package macaroni, cooked, drained	280 g
3 tablespoons oil	45 ml
1½ pounds lean ground beef, browned, drained	680 g
1 onion, chopped	
3 ribs celery, chopped	
2 (10 ounce) cans tomato soup	2 (280 g)
1 (6 ounce) can tomato paste	170 g
1 teaspoon beef bouillon granules	5 ml
1 (8 ounce) package cubed Velveeta® cheese	230 g

- Toss cooked macaroni with oil to make sure macaroni does not stick. Place in sprayed slow cooker.

- Add beef, onion, celery, tomato soup, tomato paste, beef bouillon and ⅔ cup (150 ml) water and stir to mix well.

- Cover and cook on LOW for 3 to 5 hours. Stir in cubed cheese and cook for additional 1 hour. Serves 4 to 6.

Cheeseburger in a Pot

1 (5 ounce) box bacon-cheddar scalloped potatoes	145 g
⅓ cup milk	75 ml
¼ cup (½ stick) butter, melted	60 g
1½ pounds lean ground beef	680 g
1 onion, coarsely chopped	
Canola oil	
1 (15 ounce) can whole kernel corn with liquid	425 g
1 (8 ounce) package shredded cheddar cheese	230 g

- Place scalloped potatoes in sprayed slow cooker.

- Pour 2¼ cups (560 ml) boiling water, milk and butter over potatoes.

- Brown ground beef and onion in little oil in skillet, drain and spoon over potatoes. Top with corn.

- Cover and cook on LOW for 6 to 7 hours.

- When ready to serve, sprinkle cheese over top. Serves 4 to 6.

Cowboy Round-Up

1½ pounds lean ground beef	680 g
2 onions, coarsely chopped	
5 medium potatoes, peeled, sliced	
1 (15 ounce) can kidney beans, rinsed, drained	425 g
1 (15 ounce) can pinto beans, drained	425 g
1 (15 ounce) can Mexican stewed tomatoes	425 g
1 (10 ounce) can tomato soup	280 g
½ teaspoon basil	2 ml
½ teaspoon oregano	2 ml
2 teaspoons minced garlic	10 ml

- Brown beef in skillet and sprinkle with a little salt and pepper. Drain.

- Place onions in sprayed slow cooker and spoon beef over onions.

- On top of beef, layer potatoes, kidney beans and pinto beans.

- Pour stewed tomatoes and tomato soup over beans and potatoes and sprinkle with basil, oregano and garlic.

- Cover and cook on LOW for 7 to 8 hours. Serves 4 to 6.

Fiesta Beef Patties

1½ pounds lean ground beef	680 g
1 (15 ounce) can Mexican stewed tomatoes	425 g
1 (7 ounce) box beef-flavored rice mix	200 g
1 (11 ounce) can Mexicorn®, drained	310 g
Salsa	

- Sprinkle a little salt and pepper over ground beef and shape into small patties.

- Place in sprayed 5-quart (5 L) oval slow cooker.

- Combine stewed tomatoes, rice, corn and 2 cups (500 ml) water in bowl and mix well. Spoon over beef patties.

- Cover and cook on LOW for 4 to 5 hours.

- When ready to serve, place large spoonful of salsa on each serving. Serves 4 to 6.

Beefy Hash Brown Supper

1½ pounds lean ground chuck, browned	680 g
1 (1 ounce) packet brown gravy mix	30 g
1 (15 ounce) can cream-style corn	425 g
1 (15 ounce) can whole kernel corn	425 g
1 (8 ounce) package shredded cheddar cheese, divided	230 g
1 (16 ounce) package frozen hash browns, partially thawed	455 g
1 (10 ounce) can golden mushroom soup	280 g
1 (5 ounce) can evaporated milk	150 ml

- Place browned beef in sprayed slow cooker and toss with brown gravy mix.

- Add cream-style corn and whole kernel corn and cover with half cheddar cheese.

- Top with hash browns and remaining cheese.

- Combine soup and evaporated milk in bowl. Mix well and pour over hash browns and cheese.

- Cover and cook on LOW for 6 to 8 hours. Serves 4 to 6.

Meatloaf Special

2 pounds lean ground beef	**910 g**
2 eggs, beaten	
½ cup chili sauce	**135 g**
1¼ cups seasoned breadcrumbs	**150 g**
1 (8 ounce) package shredded Monterey Jack cheese, divided	**230 g**

- Make foil handles in slow cooker. (See Turkey Loaf recipe on page 196.)

- Combine beef, eggs, chili sauce and breadcrumbs in bowl and mix well.

- Shape half beef mixture into flat loaf and place on foil "handles" in sprayed slow cooker.

- Sprinkle half cheese over meat loaf and press into meat.

- Form remaining meat mixture into same shape as first layer, place over cheese and seal seams.

- Cover and cook on LOW for 6 to 7 hours.

- When ready to serve, sprinkle remaining cheese over loaf and leave in cooker until cheese melts.

- Carefully remove loaf with foil "handles" and place on serving plate. Serves 4 to 6.

Meatloaf Surprise

1½ - 2 pounds lean ground beef	680 - 910 g
1 (1 ounce) packet beefy onion soup mix	30 g
⅔ cup quick-cooking oats	55 g
2 eggs	
1 (12 ounce) bottle chili sauce, divided	340 g

- Make foil handles in slow cooker. (See Turkey Loaf recipe on page 196.)

- Combine beef, soup mix, oats, eggs, half chili sauce and 1 teaspoon (5 ml) pepper in bowl and mix well.

- Shape meat mixture into round ball, place on foil strips in sprayed 5 to 6-quart (5 to 6 L) slow cooker and pat down into loaf shape.

- Cover and cook on LOW for 2 hours 30 minutes to 3 hours 30 minutes.

- Spread remaining chili sauce over top of loaf and continue cooking for additional 30 minutes..

- Use foil handles to lift meat loaf out of slow cooker. Serves 4 to 6.

Kids' Mac & Cheese Supper

1½ pounds lean ground beef	**680 g**
2 (7 ounce) packages macaroni and cheese dinners	**2 (200 g)**
1 (15 ounce) can whole kernel corn, drained	**425 g**
1½ cups shredded Monterey Jack cheese	**175 g**

- Sprinkle ground beef with 1 teaspoon (5 ml) salt, brown in skillet until no longer pink and drain.

- Prepare macaroni and cheese according to package directions.

- Spoon beef, macaroni and corn into sprayed 5-quart (5 L) slow cooker and mix well.

- Cover and cook on LOW for 4 to 5 hours.

- When ready to serve, sprinkle Jack cheese over top and leave in cooker until cheese melts. Serves 4 to 6.

It is worthwhile to get up a bit earlier to throw ingredients into a slow cooker than to cook at the end of a tiring day. Do not, however, put ingredients into the liner and refrigerate overnight. Starting from "cold" will increase the cooking time.

Slow Cooker Lasagna

1 pound lean ground beef	455 g
1 onion, chopped	
½ teaspoon garlic powder	2 ml
1 (18 ounce) can spaghetti sauce	510 g
½ teaspoon ground oregano	2 ml
6 - 8 lasagna noodles, divided	
1 (12 ounce) carton cottage cheese, divided	340 g
½ cup grated parmesan cheese, divided	50 g
1 (12 ounce) package shredded mozzarella cheese, divided	340 g

- Brown ground beef and onion in large skillet. Add garlic powder, spaghetti sauce and oregano. Cook just until thoroughly hot.

- Spoon half meat sauce in sprayed, oval slow cooker.

- Add layers of half lasagna noodles (break to fit slow cooker), half remaining meat sauce, half cottage cheese, half parmesan cheese and half mozzarella cheese. Repeat layers.

- Cover and cook on LOW for 6 to 8 hours. Serves 4 to 6.

Party Meatball Sauce

1 (16 ounce) can whole cranberry sauce	455 g
1 cup ketchup	270 g
⅔ cup packed brown sugar	150 g
½ cup beef broth	125 ml
1 (18 ounce) package frozen meatballs, thawed	510 g

- Combine cranberry sauce, ketchup, brown sugar and broth in sprayed, large slow cooker.

- Turn heat to HIGH and let mixture come to a boil for 30 minutes to 1 hour. Place thawed meatballs in sauce.

- Cover and cook on LOW for 2 hours.

- Remove meatballs to serving dish with slotted spoon. Insert toothpicks for easy pick up.

- Serve as appetizer, for supper or as buffet pick-up food. Serves 4 to 6.

Smothered Steak
with Mushroom Gravy

2 pounds sirloin steak or thick round steak	**910 g**
Canola oil	
1 (1 ounce) packet onion soup mix	**30 g**
1 (10 ounce) can golden mushroom soup	**280 g**
1 (4 ounce) can sliced mushrooms, drained	**115 g**
Noodles, cooked	

- Cut steak in ½-inch (1.2 cm) pieces. Brown beef in skillet in a little oil and place in sprayed 5 to 6-quart (5 to 6 L) slow cooker.

- Combine onion soup mix, mushroom soup, mushrooms and ½ cup (125 ml) water in bowl and mix well. Spoon over top of beef.

- Cover and cook on LOW for 7 to 8 hours.

- Serve over noodles. Serves 4 to 6.

Stuffed Cabbage

10 - 12 large cabbage leaves	
1½ pounds lean ground beef	**680 g**
½ cup brown rice	**95 g**
1 egg, beaten	
¼ teaspoon ground cinnamon	**1 ml**
1 (15 ounce) can tomato sauce	**425 g**

- Wash cabbage leaves, place in saucepan of boiling water and turn off heat. Soak for about 5 minutes.

- Remove leaves, drain and cool.

- Combine beef, rice, egg, 1 teaspoon (5 ml) salt, ½ teaspoon (2 ml) pepper and cinnamon in bowl and mix well.

- Place 2 tablespoons (30 ml) beef mixture on each cabbage leaf and roll tightly. (If you don't have 10 to 12 large leaves, put 2 smaller leaves together to make 1 large leaf.)

- Stack rolls in sprayed, oval slow cooker and pour tomato sauce over rolls.

- Cover and cook on HIGH for 1 hour, lower heat to LOW and cook for additional 6 to 7 hours. Serves 4 to 6.

Border Beef and Noodles

1½ pounds lean ground beef	680 g
1 (16 ounce) package frozen onions and bell peppers, thawed	455 g
1 (16 ounce) box cubed Velveeta® cheese	455 g
2 (15 ounce) cans Mexican stewed tomatoes	425 g
2 (15 ounce) cans whole kernel corn, drained	2 (425 g)
1 (8 ounce) package medium egg noodles	230 g
1 cup shredded cheddar cheese	115 g
Parsley or green onions, chopped	

- Brown ground beef in skillet and drain fat.

- Place beef in sprayed 5 to 6-quart (5 to 6 L) slow cooker, add onions and bell peppers, cheese, tomatoes, corn, and about 1 teaspoon (5 ml) salt and mix well.

- Cover and cook on LOW for 4 to 5 hours.

- Cook noodles according to package direction, drain and fold into beef-tomato mixture.

- Cook for additional 30 minutes until thoroughly hot.

- When ready to serve, top with cheddar cheese, several sprinkles of parsley or green onions. Serves 4 to 6.

Great Taste Short Ribs and Gravy

4 pounds beef short ribs   **1.8 kg**
1 onion, sliced
1 (12 ounce) jar beef gravy   **340 g**
1 (1 ounce) packet beef gravy mix   **30 g**

- Place beef ribs in sprayed 6-quart (6 L) slow cooker.

- Cover with onion and sprinkle with 1 teaspoon (5 ml) pepper.

- Combine beef gravy and gravy mix in bowl and pour over ribs and onion.

- Cover and cook on LOW for 9 to 11 hours. (The ribs must cook this long on LOW to tenderize.) Serves 4 to 6.

TIP: Serve with hot mashed potatoes.

Corned Beef Brisket

2 onions, sliced
Lemon pepper
1 (3 - 4 pound) seasoned corned beef   **1.4 - 1.8 kg**

- Place sliced onions in sprayed, large slow cooker. Add 1 cup (250 ml) water.

- Sprinkle lemon pepper liberally over corned beef and place beef on top of onion.

- Cover and cook on LOW for 7 to 9 hours.

- Remove corned beef from slow cooker and place in ovenproof pan.

- Preheat oven to 375° (190° C).

Glaze:

¼ cup honey   **85 g**
¼ cup frozen orange juice concentrate, thawed   **60 ml**
1 tablespoon mustard   **15 ml**

- Combine all glaze ingredients in bowl and spoon over corned beef.

- Bake for 30 minutes and baste occasionally with glaze before serving. Serves 6 to 8.

Shredded Brisket Sandwiches

2 teaspoons onion powder	10 ml
1 teaspoon minced garlic	5 ml
1 tablespoon liquid smoke	15 ml
1 (3 - 4 pound) beef brisket	1.4 - 1.8 kg
1 (16 ounce) bottle barbecue sauce	455 g
Kaiser rolls or hamburger buns	

- Combine onion powder, minced garlic and liquid smoke in bowl and rub over brisket.

- Place brisket in sprayed, large slow cooker. Add ⅓ cup (75 ml) water.

- Cover and cook on LOW for 6 to 8 hours or until brisket is tender.

- Remove brisket, cool and set aside ½ cup (125 ml) cooking juices.

- Shred brisket with 2 forks and place in large saucepan. Add reserved ½ cup (125 ml) cooking juices and barbecue sauce and heat thoroughly.

- Make sandwiches with kaiser rolls or hamburger buns. Serves 6 to 8.

Easy Brisket with Gravy

1 (3 - 4 pound) trimmed beef brisket	1.4 - 1.8 kg
¼ cup chili sauce	70 g
1 (1 ounce) packet herb-garlic soup mix	30 g
2 tablespoons Worcestershire sauce	30 ml
3 tablespoons cornstarch	25 g
Mashed potatoes	

- Place beef brisket in sprayed 5 to 6-quart (5 to 6 L) slow cooker. Cut to fit if necessary.

- Combine chili sauce, soup mix, Worcestershire and 1½ cups (375 ml) water and pour over brisket.

- Cover and cook on LOW for 9 to 11 hours.

- Remove brisket and keep warm. Pour juices into 2-cup (500 ml) glass measuring cup and skim fat.

- Combine cornstarch and ¼ cup (60 ml) water in saucepan. Add 1½ cups (375 ml) juices and cook, while stirring constantly, until gravy thickens.

- Slice beef thinly across grain and serve with mashed potatoes and gravy. Serves 6 to 8.

Cajun Bayou Brisket

½ cup packed brown sugar	110 g
1 tablespoon Cajun seasoning	15 ml
2 teaspoons lemon pepper	10 ml
1 tablespoon Worcestershire sauce	15 ml
1 (3 - 4 pound) trimmed beef brisket	1.4 - 1.8 kg

- Combine brown sugar, seasoning, lemon pepper and Worcestershire in bowl and spread on brisket.

- Place brisket in sprayed, oval slow cooker.

- Cover and cook on LOW for 6 to 8 hours. Serves 6 to 8.

Easy Table Brisket

1 (3 - 4 pound) trimmed beef brisket, halved	1.4 - 1.8 kg
⅓ cup grape or plum jelly	110 g
1 cup ketchup	270 g
1 (1 ounce) packet onion soup mix	30 g

- Place half of brisket in sprayed slow cooker.

- Combine jelly, ketchup, onion soup mix and ¾ teaspoon (4 ml) pepper in saucepan and heat just enough to mix well. Spread half over brisket.

- Top with remaining brisket and spread remaining jelly-soup mixture over it.

- Cover and cook on LOW for 8 to 9 hours. Slice brisket and serve with cooking juices. Serves 6 to 8.

Great Smoked Brisket

1 (4 - 6 pound) trimmed brisket	1.8 - 2.7 kg
1 (4 ounce) bottle liquid smoke	120 ml
Garlic salt	
Celery salt	
Worcestershire sauce	
1 onion, chopped	
1 (6 ounce) bottle barbecue sauce	170 g

- Place brisket in large shallow dish and pour liquid smoke over top.

- Sprinkle with garlic salt and celery salt. Cover and chill overnight.

- Before cooking, drain liquid and douse brisket with Worcestershire sauce.

- Place chopped onion in sprayed slow cooker and place brisket on top of onion.

- Cover and cook on LOW for 6 to 8 hours.

- Pour barbecue sauce over brisket and cook for additional 1 hour. Serves 6 to 8.

*Tougher or cheaper cuts of meat cook better on
LOW in the slow cooker and have a better chance
of becoming tender with longer cooking times.*

Beefy Stew Supper

1 (10 ounce) can beefy mushroom soup	280 g
1 (10 ounce) can golden mushroom soup	280 g
1 (10 ounce) can French onion soup	280 g
⅓ cup seasoned breadcrumbs	40 g
2½ pounds lean beef stew meat	1.1 kg
Noodles, cooked, buttered	

- Combine soups, ½ teaspoon (2 ml) pepper, breadcrumbs and ¾ cup (175 ml) water in sprayed 6-quart (6 L) slow cooker. Stir in beef and mix well.

- Cover and cook on LOW for 8 to 9 hours.

- Serve over noodles. Serves 6 to 8.

Beef-Potato Mix

4 medium potatoes, peeled, sliced	
1¼ pounds lean ground beef, browned	570 g
1 onion, sliced	
1 (10 ounce) can cream of mushroom soup	280 g
1 (10 ounce) can vegetable beef soup	280 g

- Layer all ingredients with a little salt and pepper in sprayed, large slow cooker.

- Cover and cook on LOW for 5 to 6 hours. Serves 4 to 6.

Mom's Hometown Rump Roast

1 (4 pound) boneless rump roast	1.8 kg
½ cup flour, divided	60 g
1 (1 ounce) packet brown gravy mix	30 g
1 (1 ounce) packet beefy onion soup mix	30 g

- If necessary to fit into cooker, cut roast in half.

- Place roast in sprayed 5 to 6-quart (5 to 6 L) slow cooker and rub half of flour over roast.

- Combine remaining flour, gravy mix and soup mix in bowl, gradually add 2 cups (500 ml) water and stir until they mix well. Pour over roast.

- Cover and cook on LOW for 7 to 8 hours or until roast is tender. Serves 6 to 8.

TIP: This makes a great gravy to serve over mashed potatoes. Use instant mashed potatoes. They will never know the difference and will love the meal!

■ ■
■   *Do not use meats that are still frozen because they may not cook*   ■
■   *thoroughly; this is not a problem with frozen vegetables.*   ■
■ ■

Soda Can Roast

1 (4 pound) chuck roast	1.8 kg
1 (12 ounce) bottle chili sauce	340 g
1 onion, chopped	
1 (12 ounce) can cola	340 g
1 tablespoon Worcestershire sauce	15 ml

- Score roast in several places and fill each slit with a little salt and pepper.

- Sear roast on all sides in skillet. Place in sprayed 5-quart (5 L) slow cooker.

- Combine chili sauce, chopped onion, cola and Worcestershire in bowl and mix well. Pour over roast.

- Cover and cook on LOW for 8 to 9 hours. Serves 6 to 8.

Basic Beef Roast

1 (3 - 4 pound) beef chuck roast	1.4 - 1.8 kg
1 (1 ounce) packet onion soup mix	30 g
2 (10 ounce) cans golden onion soup	2 (280 g)
3 - 4 medium potatoes, quartered	

- Place roast in sprayed, large slow cooker.

- Sprinkle soup mix on roast and spoon on golden onion soup. Place potatoes around roast.

- Cover and cook on LOW for 7 to 8 hours or on HIGH for 4 hours. Serves 6 to 8.

Herb-Crusted Beef Roast

1 (2 pound) beef rump roast	910 g
¼ cup chopped fresh parsley	15 g
¼ cup chopped fresh oregano leaves	15 g
½ teaspoon dried rosemary leaves	2 ml
1 teaspoon minced garlic	5 ml
1 tablespoon olive oil	15 ml
6 slices thick-cut bacon	

- Rub roast with a little salt and pepper.

- Combine parsley, oregano, rosemary, garlic and oil in small bowl and press mixture on top and sides of roast.

- Place roast in sprayed slow cooker. Place bacon over top of beef and tuck ends under bottom.

- Cover and cook on LOW for 6 to 8 hours. Serves 4 to 6.

Mushroom-Beef Supreme

2 (10 ounce) cans golden mushroom soup	2 (280 g)
1 (14 ounce) can beef broth	395 g
1 tablespoon beef seasoning	15 ml
2 (4 ounce) cans sliced mushrooms, drained	2 (115 g)
2 pounds round steak, sliced	910 g
Noodles, cooked, buttered	
1 (8 ounce) carton sour cream	230 g

- Combine soup, beef broth, beef seasoning and sliced mushrooms. Place in slow cooker and stir to blend.

- Add slices of beef and stir well.

- Cover and cook on LOW for 4 to 5 hours.

- Stir sour cream into sauce in slow cooker. Spoon sauce and beef over noodles. Serves 4 to 6.

Old-Fashioned Pot Roast

1 (2 pound) boneless rump roast	910 g
5 medium potatoes, peeled, quartered	
1 (16 ounce) package baby carrots	455 g
2 medium onions, quartered	
1 (10 ounce) can golden mushroom soup	280 g
½ teaspoon dried basil	2 ml
½ teaspoon seasoned salt	2 ml

- Brown roast on all sides in large non-stick skillet.

- Place potatoes, carrots and onions in sprayed 4 to 5-quart (4 to 5 L) slow cooker.

- Place browned roast on top of vegetables.

- Combine soup, basil and seasoned salt in bowl and pour mixture over meat and vegetables.

- Cover and cook on LOW for 9 to 11 hours. Serves 4 to 6.

TIP: To serve, transfer roast and vegetables to serving plate. Stir juices remaining in slow cooker and spoon over roast and vegetables.

Large or firm vegetables like potatoes, onions and carrots cook more slowly than meat. Put these vegetables in the slow cooker first and put the meat on top of them.

Savory Beef Roast

1 (2 pound) boneless chuck roast	**910 g**
½ cup flour	**60 g**
Canola oil	
1 onion, sliced	
½ cup chili sauce	**135 g**
¾ cup packed brown sugar	**165 g**
¼ cup red wine vinegar	**60 ml**
1 tablespoon Worcestershire sauce	**15 ml**
1 (16 ounce) package peeled baby carrots	**455 g**

- Cut beef into 1-inch cubes and dredge in flour mixed with a little salt and pepper.

- Brown beef in a little oil in skillet and place in sprayed slow cooker.

- Combine remaining ingredients, except carrots, and 1 cup (250 ml) water. Pour over beef.

- Cover and cook on LOW for 7 to 8 hours.

- Add carrots and cook for additional 1 hour 30 minutes. Serves 4 to 6.

Sunday Roast and Potatoes

1 (2 pound) chuck roast	910 g
4 - 5 medium potatoes, peeled, quartered	
4 large carrots, quartered	
1 onion, quartered	
1 (14 ounce) can beef broth, divided	395 g
2 tablespoons cornstarch	15 g

- Trim fat from pieces of roast. Cut roast into 2 equal pieces.

- Brown pieces of roast in skillet. (Coat pieces with flour, salt and pepper if you like a little "breading" on the outside.)

- Place potatoes, carrots and onion in sprayed 4 to 5-quart (4 to 5 L) slow cooker and mix well. Place browned beef over vegetables.

- Pour 1½ cups (375 ml) broth over beef and vegetables. Refrigerate remaining broth.

- Cover and cook on LOW for 8 to 9 hours. About 5 minutes before serving, remove beef and vegetables with slotted spoon and place on serving platter. Cover to keep warm.

- Pour liquid from slow cooker into medium saucepan.

- Blend remaining broth and cornstarch in bowl until smooth and add to liquid in saucepan. Boil for 1 minute and stir constantly.

- Serve gravy with roast and veggies and season with a little salt and pepper, if desired. Serves 4 to 6.

Quick Pasta and Beef Tips

2 pounds lean, beef stew meat	910 g
2 cups frozen, small whole onions, thawed	370 g
1 green bell pepper, seeded, cut in 1-inch (2.54 cm) pieces	
1 (6 ounce) jar pitted Greek olives or ripe olives	170 g
½ cup sun-dried tomatoes in oil, drained, chopped	30 g
1 (28 ounce) jar marinara sauce	795 g
1 (8 ounce) package pasta twirls, cooked	230 g

- Place beef and onions in sprayed 4 to 5-quart (4 to 5 L) slow cooker.

- Cut bell pepper in 1-inch (2.5 cm) cubes and add to slow cooker.

- Add olives and tomatoes and pour marinara sauce over top.

- Cover and cook on LOW for 8 to 10 hours.

- Serve over pasta twirls. Serves 4 to 6.

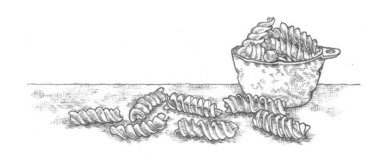

Favorite Beef Tips over Noodles

3 pounds beef tips	1.4 kg
½ cup plus 3 tablespoons flour, divided	80 g
1 (8 ounce) carton fresh mushrooms, sliced	230 g
1 bunch green onions, chopped	
1 small red bell pepper, seeded, chopped	
¼ cup ketchup	70 g
1 (14 ounce) can beef broth	395 g
1 tablespoon Worcestershire sauce	15 ml
Noodles, cooked, buttered	

- Coat beef tips with ½ cup (60 g) flour in bowl and transfer to sprayed slow cooker.

- Add mushrooms, onion, bell pepper, ketchup, broth, Worcestershire sauce and a little salt and pepper.

- Cover and cook on LOW for 7 to 8 hours. Turn heat to HIGH and cook additional 1 hour.

- Combine remaining flour with ¼ cup (60 ml) water in small bowl, stir into cooker and cook until liquid thickens.

- Serve over noodles. Serves 6 to 8.

Beef Roulades

1½ pounds beef flank steak	680 g
5 slices bacon	
¾ cup finely chopped onion	120 g
1 (4 ounce) can mushroom pieces	115 g
1 tablespoon Worcestershire sauce	15 ml
⅓ cup Italian-seasoned breadcrumbs	40 g
1 (12 ounce) jar beef gravy	340 g

- Cut steak into 4 to 6 serving-size pieces.

- With kitchen shears, cut bacon into small pieces and combine with onion, mushrooms, Worcestershire and breadcrumbs in bowl.

- Divide onion mixture evenly and place on each piece of steak.

- Roll meat and secure ends with wooden toothpicks. Dry roulades (rolls) with paper towels.

- Brown roulades in skillet and transfer to sprayed slow cooker.

- Pour gravy evenly over roulades to thoroughly moisten.

- Cover and cook on LOW for 7 to 9 hours. Serves 4 to 6.

TIP: This is really good served with mashed potatoes. Have you tried instant mashed potatoes as a time-saver?

Dive-In Beefy-Onion Supper

1 - 1½ pounds round steak	455 - 680 g
1 onion	
2 cups fresh sliced mushrooms	145 g
1 (10 ounce) can French onion soup	280 g
1 (6 ounce) package herb stuffing mix	170 g
½ cup (1 stick) butter, melted	115 g

- Cut beef into 5 to 6 serving-size pieces.

- Slice onion and separate into rings.

- Place steak pieces in sprayed, oval slow cooker and top with mushrooms and onions.

- Pour soup over ingredients in cooker.

- Cover and cook on LOW for 7 to 9 hours.

- Just before serving, combine stuffing mix with seasoning packet, butter and ½ cup (125 ml) liquid from cooker in bowl and toss to mix.

- Place stuffing mixture on top of steak and increase heat to HIGH.

- Cover and cook for additional 15 minutes or until stuffing is fluffy. Serves 4 to 6.

Surprise Steak Italian

1 pound round steak, cubed	455 g
2 cups fresh mushroom halves	145 g
1 (15 ounce) can Italian stewed tomatoes	425 g
1 (14 ounce) can beef broth	395 g
½ cup red wine	125 ml
2 teaspoons Italian seasoning	10 ml
3 tablespoons quick-cooking tapioca	30 g
Linguine, cooked, buttered	

- Place beef in sprayed 4 to 5-quart (4 to 5 L) slow cooker.

- Combine mushrooms, tomatoes, beef broth, wine, Italian seasoning, tapioca and a little salt and pepper in bowl. Pour over steak.

- Cover and cook on LOW for 8 to 10 hours. Serve over linguine. Serves 4.

Mushroom-Onion Steak

1½ - 2 pounds round steak	680 - 910 g
1 (1 ounce) packet onion soup mix	30 g
½ cup dry red wine	125 ml
1 (8 ounce) carton fresh mushrooms, sliced	230 g
1 (10 ounce) can French onion soup	280 g

- Cut round steak in serving-size pieces and place in sprayed, oval slow cooker.

- Combine soup mix, wine, mushrooms, soup and ½ cup (125 ml) water in bowl; spoon over steak pieces.

- Cover and cook on LOW for 7 to 8 hours. Serves 4 to 6.

Teriyaki Flank

1½ - 2 pounds flank steak	680 - 910 g
1 (15 ounce) can sliced pineapple with juice	425 g
1 tablespoon marinade for chicken	15 ml
⅓ cup packed brown sugar	75 g
3 tablespoons soy sauce	45 ml
½ teaspoon ground ginger	2 ml
1 (14 ounce) can chicken broth	395 g
1 cup rice	185 g

- Roll flank steak, tie and cut into 7 to 8 individual steaks.

- Combine ½ cup (125 ml) pineapple juice, marinade for chicken, brown sugar, soy sauce and ginger in bowl

- Marinate steaks for 1 hour. Drain and discard marinade.

- Pour chicken broth into sprayed slow cooker.

- Add rice and ¾ cup (175 ml) water. Place steaks over rice and broth.

- Cover and cook on LOW for 8 to 10 hours. Uncover and add pineapple slices; cook for additional 15 minutes. Serves 4 to 6.

Simple Stroganoff

2 pounds beef round steak	910 g
¾ cup flour, divided	90 g
½ teaspoon dry mustard	2 ml
2 onions, thinly sliced	
½ pound fresh mushrooms, sliced	230 g
1 (10 ounce) can beef broth	280 g
¼ cup dry white wine or cooking wine	60 ml
1 (8 ounce) carton sour cream	230 g

- Trim excess fat from steak and cut into 3-inch (8 cm) strips about ½-inch (1.2 cm) wide.

- Combine ½ cup (60 g) flour, mustard and a little salt and pepper in bowl and toss with steak strips.

- Place strips in sprayed, oval slow cooker.

- Cover with onions and mushrooms. Add beef broth and wine.

- Cover and cook on LOW for 8 to 10 hours.

- Just before serving, combine sour cream and ¼ cup (30 g) flour in bowl.

- Stir into cooker and cook for additional 10 to 15 minutes or until stroganoff thickens slightly. Serves 4 to 6.

Cross-the-Border Swiss Steak

1½ pounds boneless beef round steak	680 g
4 ounces spicy bratwurst, sliced	115 g
2 small onions	
2 tablespoons quick-cooking tapioca	20 g
1 teaspoon dried thyme	5 ml
2 (15 ounce) cans Mexican stewed tomatoes	2 (425 g)
Noodles, cooked	

- Trim fat from steak and cut into 4 serving-size pieces.

- Brown steak and bratwurst in skillet. Drain and place in sprayed 4 to 5-quart (4 to 5 L) slow cooker.

- Slice onions and separate into rings.

- Cover meat with onions and sprinkle with tapioca, thyme, and a little salt and pepper. Pour stewed tomatoes over onion and seasonings.

- Cover and cook on LOW for 5 to 8 hours.

- Serve over noodles. Serves 4 to 6.

Simple Swiss Steak

1 - 1½ pounds boneless, round steak	680 - 910 g
½ teaspoon seasoned salt	2 ml
½ teaspoon seasoned pepper	2 ml
8 - 10 medium new (red) potatoes with peels, halved	
1 cup baby carrots	135 g
1 onion, sliced	
1 (15 ounce) can stewed tomatoes	425 g
1 (12 ounce) jar beef gravy	340 g

- Cut steak in 6 to 8 serving-size pieces, sprinkle with seasoned salt and pepper and brown in non-stick skillet.

- Layer steak pieces, potatoes, carrots and onion in sprayed slow cooker.

- Combine tomatoes and beef gravy in bowl and spoon over vegetables.

- Cover and cook on LOW for 7 to 8 hours. Serves 4 to 6.

Beefy Pepper Steak

1½ pounds round steak	680 g
Canola oil	
¼ cup soy sauce	60 ml
1 onion, sliced	
1 teaspoon minced garlic	5 ml
1 teaspoon sugar	5 ml
¼ teaspoon ground ginger	1 ml
1 (15 ounce) can stewed tomatoes	425 g
2 green bell peppers, seeded, julienned	
1 teaspoon beef bouillon granules	5 ml
1 tablespoon cornstarch	15 ml
Rice or noodles, cooked, buttered	

- Slice beef in strips, brown in skillet with a little oil and place in sprayed, oval slow cooker.

- Combine soy sauce, onion, garlic, sugar and ginger in bowl and pour over beef.

- Cover and cook on LOW for 5 to 6 hours.

- Add tomatoes, bell peppers and bouillon and cook for additional 1 hour.

- Combine cornstarch and ¼ cup water (60 ml) in cup and stir into cooker. Continue cooking until liquid thickens.

- Serve over rice or noodles. Serves 4 to 6.

Smothered Steak

Great sauce for mashed potatoes

1½ pounds lean round steak	680 g
1 onion, halved, sliced	
2 (10 ounce) cans golden mushroom soup	2 (280 g)
1½ cups hot, thick-and-chunky salsa	395 g

- Trim fat from steak and cut into serving-size pieces. Sprinkle with 1 teaspoon (5 ml) pepper and place in sprayed 5 to 6-quart (5 to 6 L) slow cooker. Place onion slices over steak.

- Combine mushroom soup and salsa in bowl and mix well. Spoon over steak and onions.

- Cover and cook on LOW for 7 to 8 hours. Serves 4 to 6.

Beef in a Pot

3 cups cooked, cubed roast beef	420 g
1 (28 ounce) package frozen hash browns with	
onions and peppers, thawed	795 g
Canola oil	
1 (16 ounce) jar salsa	455 g
1 tablespoon beef seasoning	15 ml
1 cup shredded cheddar-Jack cheese	115 g

- Place beef in sprayed, large slow cooker.

- Brown potatoes in a little oil in large skillet. Stir in salsa and beef seasoning and transfer to slow cooker. Cover and cook on HIGH for 4 to 5 hours.

- When ready to serve, sprinkle cheese over top. Serves 4.

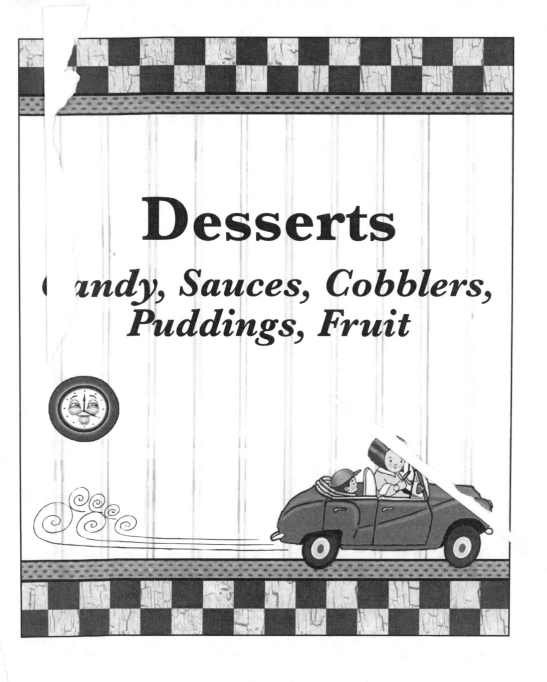

Desserts

Candy, Sauces, Cobblers, Puddings, Fruit

Sweets Contents

There is a time every day when the phones are quiet, the
TV is off and e-mails will wait until later. For a few moments,
you are not a student or an executive, at a PTA meeting or
on a sales call. Now, you are family. This is dinnertime.

Fudge Almighty

2 (16 ounce) jars slightly salted, dry-roasted peanuts   **2 (455 g)**
1 (12 ounce) package semi-sweet chocolate chips   **340 g**
1 (4 ounce) bar German chocolate, broken   **115 g**
2 (24 ounce) packages white chocolate bark or
   3 pounds almond bark, chopped   **2 (680 g)/1.4 kg**

- Place peanuts in sprayed 5-qu   vers, add
  chocolate chips, German choc

- Cover and cook on LOW for 3 hours without removing lid.

- When candy has cooked 3 hours, remove lid, stir and cool in covered
  slow cooker.

- Stir again and drop teaspoons of mixture onto wax paper.
  Yields 5 pounds (2.3 kg) fudge.

TIP: For darker fudge, use 1 white bark and 1 dark bark. DO NOT STIR
    until candy has cooked 3 hours.

Cran-Apples Spectacular

1 (6 ounce) package dried apples	170 g
½ cup Craisins®	60 g
3 cups cranberry juice cocktail	750 ml
¾ cup packed brown sugar	165 g
2 cinnamon sticks, halved	

- Add apples, Craisins®, juice, brown sugar and cinnamon sticks to sprayed 3 to 4-quart (3 to 4 L) slow cooker.

- Cover and cook on LOW for 4 to 5 hours or until liquid absorbs and fruit is tender.

- Serve warm, at room temperature or chilled over slices of pound cake or vanilla ice cream. Serves 6.

Fruity Dessert Sauce

8 cups fresh fruit, thinly sliced	1.2 - 1.5 kg
1 cup orange juice	250 ml
⅓ cup packed brown sugar	75 g
⅓ cup sugar	70 g
2 tablespoons quick-cooking tapioca	20 g
1 teaspoon grated fresh ginger	5 ml
⅔ cup dried cranberries or cherries	80 g

- Combine fruit, orange juice, brown sugar, sugar, tapioca and ginger in sprayed 4-quart (4 L) slow cooker.

- Cover and cook on LOW for 4 hours. Add dried cranberries or cherries and mix well. Cover and let stand for 10 to 15 minutes.

- To serve, spoon over slices of pound cake or ice cream. Serves 6 to 8.

Chocolate Party Fondue

Use the slow cooker as a fondue pot.

2 (7 ounce) bars chocolate, chopped	2 (200 g)
1 (4 ounce) bar white chocolate, chopped	115 g
1 (7 ounce) jar marshmallow creme	200 g
¾ cup half-and-half cream	175 ml
½ cup slivered almonds, chopped, toasted	85 g
¼ cup amaretto liqueur	60 ml
Pound cake	

- Combine chopped chocolate bars, chopped white chocolate bar, marshmallow creme, half-and-half cream and almonds in sprayed, small slow cooker.

- Cover and cook on LOW for about 2 hours or until chocolates melt.

- Stir to mix well and fold in amaretto. Serves 8 to 10.

TIP: Use slow cooker as fondue pot or transfer chocolate mixture to fondue pot. Cut pound cake into small squares and dip into fondue.

Slow Chocolate Fix

1 (18 ounce) box chocolate cake mix	510 g
1 (8 ounce) carton sour cream	230 g
4 eggs, beaten	
¾ cup canola oil	175 ml
1 (3.4 ounce) box instant chocolate pudding mix	100 g
¾ cup chopped pecans	85 g

- Combine cake mix, sour cream, eggs, oil, pudding mix, pecans and 1 cup (250 ml) water in bowl. Pour into sprayed slow cooker.

- Cover and cook on LOW for 6 to 8 hours.

- Serve hot or warm with vanilla ice cream. Serves 18.

Butterscotch-Spice Cake

1 (18 ounce) box spice cake mix	510 g
1 cup butterscotch chips	170 g
4 eggs, slightly beaten	
¾ cup canola oil	175 ml
1 (3.4 ounce) package butterscotch instant pudding mix	100 g
1 (8 ounce) carton sour cream	230 g
1 cup chopped pecans	110 g

- Combine all ingredients and ¾ cup (175 ml) water in bowl. Pour into sprayed, 4 to 5-quart (4 to 5 L) slow cooker.

- Cover and cook on LOW for 6 to 7 hours or on HIGH for 3 hours to 3 hours 30 minutes.

- Serve hot or room temperature with butter-pecan ice cream. Serves 18.

Pineapple-Rice Pudding

1 cup cooked rice	160 g
¾ cup sugar	150 g
1 (1 pint) carton half-and-half cream	500 ml
1 tablespoon cornstarch	15 ml
3 eggs, beaten	
1 teaspoon vanilla	5 ml
1 (15 ounce) can crushed pineapple with juice	425 g
Chopped pecans, toasted, optional	

- Combine rice, sugar and half-and-half cream in bowl and mix well.

- Stir in cornstarch, eggs, vanilla and pineapple.

- Pour into sprayed 4 to 5-quart (4 to 5 L) slow cooker.

- Cover and cook on LOW for 2 to 3 hours.

- When ready to serve, top each serving with toasted, chopped pecans as a special touch. Serves 6.

Fresh Peach Cobbler

1 cup sugar	200 g
¾ cup biscuit mix	90 g
2 eggs	
2 teaspoons vanilla	10 ml
1 (5 ounce) can evaporated milk	150 ml
2 tablespoons butter, melted	30 g
3 large ripe peaches, mashed	

- Combine sugar and biscuit mix in bowl, stir in egg, vanilla, evaporated milk and butter and mix well. Fold in peaches, pour into sprayed slow cooker and stir well.

- Cover and cook on LOW for 6 to 8 hours or on HIGH for 3 to 4 hours. Serve warm with peach ice cream. Serves 6 to 8.

Peach Crunch

¾ cup old-fashioned oats	60 g
⅔ cup packed brown sugar	150 g
¾ cup sugar	150 g
½ cup biscuit mix	60 g
½ teaspoon ground cinnamon	2 ml
2 (15 ounce) cans sliced peaches, well drained	2 (425 g)

- Combine oats, brown sugar, sugar, biscuit mix and cinnamon in bowl.

- Stir in drained peaches and spoon into sprayed 3 to 4-quart (3 to 4 L) slow cooker. Cover and cook on LOW for 4 to 5 hours. Serve in sherbet dishes. Serves 6 to 8.

Campfire-Baked Apples in a Pot

6 large green baking apples	
2 tablespoons lemon juice	**30 ml**
¼ cup (½ stick) butter, melted	**60 g**
1 cup packed brown sugar	**220 g**
1 teaspoon ground cinnamon	**5 ml**
½ teaspoon ground nutmeg	**2 ml**
Vanilla ice cream	

- Peel, core and halve apples and place in sprayed slow cooker.

- Drizzle with lemon juice and butter. Sprinkle with brown sugar, cinnamon and nutmeg.

- Cover and cook on LOW for 2 hours 30 minutes to 3 hours 30 minutes or on HIGH for 1 hour 30 minutes to 2 hours.

- Serve with vanilla ice cream. Serves 4 to 6.

Nutty Coconut Bread Pudding

1 cup sugar	200 g
½ cup (1 stick) butter, softened	115 g
1 teaspoon ground cinnamon	5 ml
4 eggs	
3 cups white bread cubes	105 g
⅓ cup flaked coconut	30 g
⅓ cup chopped pecans	40 g

- Beat sugar, butter and cinnamon in bowl. Add eggs and beat well until it blends.

- Stir in bread, coconut and pecans. Pour into sprayed 4 to 5-quart (4 to 5 L) slow cooker.

- Cover and cook on LOW for 3 to 4 hours or on HIGH for 1 hour 30 minutes to 2 hours or until knife inserted in center comes out clean. Serves 8.

TIP: Serve pudding warm with caramel ice cream topping, if desired.

Slow Cook Baked Apples

4 - 5 large baking apples	
1 tablespoon lemon juice	**15 ml**
⅓ cup Craisins®	**40 g**
½ cup chopped pecans	**55 g**
¾ cup packed brown sugar	**165 g**
½ teaspoon ground cinnamon	**2 ml**
¼ cup (½ stick) butter, softened	**60 g**

- Scoop out center of each apple and leave cavity about ½ inch (1.2 cm) from bottom.

- Peel top of apples down about 1 inch (2.5 cm) and brush lemon juice on peeled edges.

- Combine Craisins®, pecans, brown sugar, cinnamon and butter in bowl. Spoon mixture into apple cavities.

- Pour ½ cup (125 ml) water in sprayed, oval slow cooker and arrange apples inside.

- Cover and cook on LOW for 1 to 3 hours or until tender.

- Serve warm or at room temperature drizzled with caramel ice cream topping. Serves 4 to 5.

Delicious Bread Pudding

8 cups cubed leftover hot rolls, cinnamon rolls or bread	280 g
2 cups milk	500 ml
4 large eggs	
¾ cup sugar	150 g
⅓ cup packed brown sugar	75 g
¼ cup (½ stick) butter, melted	60 g
1 teaspoon vanilla	5 ml
¼ teaspoon nutmeg	1 ml
1 cup finely chopped pecans	110 g
Whipped topping, thawed	

- Place cubed bread or rolls in sprayed slow cooker.

- Combine milk, eggs, sugar, brown sugar, butter, vanilla and nutmeg in bowl and beat until smooth. Stir in pecans. Pour over bread.

- Cover and cook on LOW for 3 hours.

- Serve with whipped topping. Serves 8.

Appendices

U.S. and Metric Measurements, Food Substitutions, Pantry Basics, Flavored Butters, Potatoes

U.S. and Metric Measurements

Please note: In U.S. cookery, all ingredients are measured by volume. In metric measurements, dry ingredients plus some other items are measured by weight (grams and kilograms), not by volume (milliliters and liters).

Common Metric Abbreviations:

Grams	g
Kilograms	kg
Milliliters	ml
Liters	L
Millimeters	mm
Centimeters	cm

Basic Conversion Formulas

1 fluid ounce = 29.57 milliliters

1 avoirdupois ounce (weight) = 28.35 grams

continued next page...

U.S. and Metric Measurements — continued

Liquid Volume

3 teaspoons	1 tablespoon	0.5 fluid ounce	15 ml
4 tablespoons	¼ cup	2 fluid ounces	60 ml
8 tablespoons	½ cup	4 fluid ounces	125 ml
12 tablespoons	¾ cup	6 fluid ounces	175 ml
16 tablespoons	1 cup	8 fluid ounces	250 ml
¼ cup	4 tablespoons	2 fluid ounces	60 ml
⅓ cup	5 tablespoons + 1 teaspoon	2.7 fluid ounces	75 ml
½ cup	8 tablespoons	4 fluid ounces	125 ml
⅔ cup	10 tablespoons + 2 teaspoons	5.4 fluid ounces	150 ml
¾ cup	12 tablespoons	6 fluid ounces	175 ml
1 cup	16 tablespoons; ½ pint	8 fluid ounces	250 ml
2 cups	1 pint	16 fluid ounces	
3 cups	1½ pints	24 fluid ounces	
4 cups	1 quart	32 fluid ounces	
8 cups	2 quarts	64 fluid ounces	
1 pint	2 cups	16 fluid ounces	
2 pints	1 quart	32 fluid ounces	
1 quart	2 pints; 4 cups	32 fluid ounces	
4 quarts	1 gallon; 8 pints; 16 cups	64 fluid ounces	

Other Volume Measures

8 quarts . . . . 1 peck
4 pecks. . . . . 1 bushel

continued next page...

U.S. and Metric Measurements — continued

Weight Measurements

Avoirdupois Ounces	Pounds	Metric (grams)
1 ounce		30 grams
2 ounces		55 grams
3 ounces		85 grams
4 ounces	¼ pound	115 grams
5 ounces		140 grams
6 ounces		170 grams
8 ounces	½ pound	230 grams
10 ounces		280 grams
12 ounces	¼ pound	340 grams
14 ounces		395 grams
16 ounces	1 pound	455 grams
32 ounces	2 pounds	910 grams
35 ounces	2.2 pounds	1 kilogram

Distance (Length) Measurements

Inches	Centimeters
0.39 inch	1 cm
1 inch	2.54 cm
12 inches (1 foot(	30.48 cm
36 inches (3 feet)	91.44 cm
39.37 inches	1 meter (100 cm)

Food Substitutions

You Need:	Use Instead:
1 cup breadcrumbs	¾ cup cracker crumbs
1 cup butter	⅞ cup vegetable oil or shortening
1 cup buttermilk	1 cup milk plus 1 tablespoon vinegar or lemon juice; or 1 cup plain yogurt
1 ounce unsweetened chocolate	3 tablespoons unsweetened cocoa plus 1 tablespoon butter
1 tablespoon cornstarch	2 tablespoons flour
1 cup cracker crumbs	1¼ cups breadcrumbs
1 cup cake flour	1 cup, less 2 tablespoons flour
1 clove garlic	1 teaspoon garlic salt less ½ teaspoon salt in recipe
1 tablespoon fresh herbs	1 teaspoon dried herbs
1 cup whole milk	½ cup evaporated milk plus ½ cup water; or ¾ cup nonfat milk plus ¼ cup butter
1 tablespoon prepared mustard	1 teaspoon dry mustard
1 small onion	1 tablespoon minced onion; or ½ teaspoon onion powder
1 cup sour cream	1 cup plain yogurt; or 1 tablespoon lemon juice plus enough evaporated whole milk to equal 1 cup
1 cup sugar	1¾ cups powdered sugar; or 1 cup packed brown sugar
1 cup powdered sugar	½ cup plus 1 tablespoon granulated sugar
1 cup tomato juice	½ cup tomato sauce plus ½ cup water
1 cup tomato sauce	½ cup tomato paste plus ½ cup water
1 cup yogurt	1 cup milk plus 1 tablespoon lemon juice

Pantry Basics

Most folks will not want every item, but this can help you decide what to keep on hand for easy meals and ordinary needs.

You may also want to keep about a 3 to 4 day supply of bottled water and food that does not need to be cooked for emergencies. You can rotate this supply into your regular pantry so that items do not pass their expiration dates.

Convenience foods are great to have when you're in a hurry to get something on the table. You can even make your own "instant" meals and freeze or refrigerate for later use.

Here are some suggestions for basics to keep in your pantry:

Canned Savory Foods

Keep a supply of whole and chopped tomatoes; beans; vegetables such as corn, asparagus, and artichoke hearts; tuna; cooked ham; sauces; condensed and ready-to–heat soups; peanut and other nut butters.

Canned Sweet Foods

Store canned fruits such as pineapple (chunks and slices); pears; peach halves or slices; exotic fruits such as litchis and guavas; fruit pie fillings; applesauce; and fruit cocktail.

continued next page…

Pantry Basics — continued

Dry Foods and Packaged Mixes

Stock sauce and gravy mixes; dried vegetables; instant mashed potatoes; pasta and rice mixes; instant desserts; instant nonfat dry milk and gelatin powder; bread, pastry, batter, and cake mixes.

Bottled Foods and Preserves

Keep jams and jellies; fruits in brandy; ready-made meals such as chili or baked beans; pesto; olives; sun-dried tomatoes; and antipasto.

Prepared Foods

Stock up with partly baked breads and pastries; prepared ready-to-serve meals and pasta dishes; milk, cream, and whipped desserts.

Refrigerated Foods

Refrigerated prepared meals; fresh pasta; soups; sweet and savory sauces; fruit salad; prepared mixed salads and dressings; fresh pastry; and dips.

continued next page...

Pantry Basics — continued

Frozen Savory Foods

Frozen vegetables and stir-fry mixes; French fries; cooked rice; pizza bases; prepared fish and shellfish; meat and poultry; pastry, pies, and quiches.

Frozen Sweet Foods

Frozen prepared fruits, especially raspberries and seasonal soft-fruit mixes; melon balls; ices, sorbets, and iced desserts; cakes; and fruit juices.

Basic Seasonings & Flavorings

Spices, herbs and condiments are easy ways to add flavor to the simplest dishes and convenience foods. Keep basics on hand such as jams and preserves, ketchup, mayonnaise, mustard, peanut butter, pickles, vinegar, salsa, hot red pepper sauce. Some of the most common spices and herbs include chili powder, cinnamon, cumin, dill weed, garlic powder, dried minced onions, Italian seasoning, seasoned salt, paprika, oregano, thyme, chives, salt, and pepper.

Basic Baking Supplies

Be sure to keep common baking supplies on hand: flour, sugar, brown sugar, powdered sugar, baking powder, baking soda, yeast, shortening and oils, cooking spray, chocolate chips, nuts, And don't forget convenient mixes, refrigerated cookies and dinner rolls, and biscuits.

Flavored Butters

F lavored butters are an easy way to add excitement to a meal, but are usually forgotten in the rush to get a meal prepared. Most flavored butters can be made ahead of time and either stored in the refrigerator or frozen for later use.

Flavored butters can be added to meats or fish, melted into vegetable dishes or potatoes, or used with breads and biscuits to add fruit flavors or sweetness. They can be made in minutes, and they can make a big difference in flavor and texture of foods.

How to Make Flavored Butter

Basically, flavored butter is made by combining softened butter with your favorite herbs, spices, fruits, sauces, etc., to create the taste you want. The best texture is created when you beat the butter until it is fluffy.

An easy way to store flavored butter is to roll the mixture into a "log" and then wrap it up tightly to store it in the refrigerator for as much as week. To freeze, secure the "log" by wrapping it tightly in foil, and placing it in the freezer for as much as one month.

The butter tends to lose its flavor, so don't forget it's in there. Flavored butters can be sliced when frozen and added directly to hot meats or vegetables.

Be sure to set refrigerated butter out for 15 minutes before serving to allow it to soften.

continued next page...

Flavored Butters — continued

Garlic Butter

½ cup (1 stick) butter,
   softened   115 g
2 cloves of garlic, minced
2 tablespoons chopped
   parsley   10 g

- Mix all ingredients in a bowl
  until they blend well. Use on
  vegetables, rice, breads, and
  grilled or broiled fish and meats.
  Try it on lamb chops or the next
  time you grill salmon.

Mustard Butter

½ cup (1 stick) butter,
   softened   115 g
¼ teaspoon garlic salt   1 ml
½ teaspoon Worcestershire
   sauce   1ml
2 tablespoons chopped
   fresh parsley   10 g
2 teaspoons dry mustard   10 ml

- Mix all ingredients with a little
  pepper in a bowl until they
  blend well. Use on meats, fish,
  sandwiches or vegetables.

Fruit Butter

½ cup (1 stick) unsalted
   butter, softened   115 g
1 (8 ounce) package cream
   cheese, softened   230 g
1 cup preserves or jam   320 g

- Beat butter and cream cheese
  together until smooth. Add
  preserves or jam and mix until
  they blend well. (Use apricot or
  strawberry preserves or orange
  marmalade or your favorite
  flavor.)

Parmesan Butter

½ cup (1 stick) butter,
   softened   115 g
2 tablespoons grated
   parmesan or romano
   cheese   15 g
2 teaspoons minced green
   onions   10 ml

- Combine all ingredients until
  they blend well. Use on
  vegetables or breads.

continued next page...

Flavored Butters — continued

Cheese Butter

½ cup (1 stick) butter,
   softened   115 g
1 cup finely shredded
   cheese   115 g
½ teaspoon Worcestershire
   sauce   1 ml
¼ teaspoon garlic powder   1 ml
½ teaspoon Italian
   seasoning   1 ml

- Combine all ingredients with
  a little pepper. (Use Swiss,
  cheddar, or your favorite cheese.)

Citrus Butter

½ cup (1 stick) butter,
   softened   115 g
2 teaspoons lemon juice   10 ml
2 teaspoons lime juice   10 ml
4 teaspoons orange juice 20 ml
¾ teaspoon dried tarragon 4 ml
¾ teaspoon dried basil   4 ml

- Combine all ingredients with
  a little pepper until smooth.
  Yummy on hot biscuits, muffins
  or toast.

Herb Butter

½ cup (1 stick) butter,
   softened   115 g
2 teaspoons minced fresh
   parsley   10 ml
½ teaspoon tarragon   2 ml
1 teaspoon dry mustard 5 ml

- Combine all ingredients until
  they blend well. Use on
  vegetables or on meats or fish.
  Other good combinations for
  herb butter include: basil and
  chives; onion and garlic; sage,
  rosemary and thyme; mint and
  lemon; sage and onion.

Bacon Butter

½ cup (1 stick) butter,
   softened   115 g
½ teaspoon oregano   2 ml
4 strips bacon, cooked
   crisp, crumbled

- Combine all ingredients with a
  little pepper. Use on potatoes
  and vegetables.

continued next page...

Flavored Butters — continued

Butter for Meats

½ cup (1 stick) butter, softened	115 g
1 teaspoon seasoned salt	5 ml
⅛ teaspoon garlic powder	.5 ml
⅛ teaspoon hot pepper sauce	.5 ml
1 teaspoon liquid smoke	5 ml
1 tablespoon Worcestershire sauce	15 ml
2 tablespoons steak sauce	30 ml

- Combine all ingredients until they blend well. Use on beef, pork or chicken.

Strawberry Butter

½ cup (1 stick) butter, softened	115 g
2 tablespoons powdered sugar	15 g
½ cup mashed fresh strawberries or other berries	115 g

- Combine butter and powdered sugar until they blend well. Add mashed strawberries and mix well.

Apple Pie Flavored Butter

½ cup (1 stick) butter, softened	115 g
2 tablespoons apple preserves or apple pie filling	40 g
⅛ teaspoon ground cinnamon	.5 ml
Pinch of ground nutmeg	

- Combine all ingredients until they blend well. Delicious with muffins or other breads.

Cinnamon Sugar Butter

½ cup (1 stick) butter, softened	115 g
¾ cup sugar	150 g
1 tablespoon cinnamon	15 ml

- Combine all ingredients until they blend well. Use on toast, biscuits or bagels.

continued next page...

Flavored Butters — continued

Brown Sugar-Maple Butter

½ cup (1 stick) butter,	
softened	115 g
2 tablespoons brown sugar	30 g
2 tablespoons pure maple	
syrup	30 ml

- Combine all ingredients until they blend well.

Honey Nut Butter

½ cup (1 stick) butter,	
softened	115 g
2 tablespoons honey	45 g
3 tablespoons finely	
chopped nuts	55 g

- Combine all ingredients until they blend well.

Honey-Almond Butter

½ cup (1 stick) butter,	
softened	115 g
1 tablespoon honey	15 ml
¼ teaspoon almond extract	1 ml

- Combine all ingredients until they blend well.

Honey-Orange Butter

½ cup (1 stick) butter,	
softened	115 g
2 tablespoons honey	45 g
2 tablespoons orange	
marmalade	40 g
1 tablespoon orange zest	15 ml
⅛ teaspoon vanilla	.5 ml

- Combine all ingredients until they blend well.

Lemon or Lime Butter

½ cup (1 stick) butter,	
softened	115 g
2 tablespoons minced fresh	
parsley	10 g
4 teaspoons lemon or	
lime juice	20 ml

- Combine all ingredients until they blend well. Use with fish or vegetables. For extra spice, add a little cayenne pepper.

continued next page...

Flavored Butters — continued

Basil Garlic Butter

½ cup (1 stick) butter,
   softened   115 g
1 tablespoon basil   15 ml
2 cloves garlic, crushed

- Combine all ingredients with a little salt until they blend well.

Herb Butter for Seafood

½ cup (1 stick) butter,
   softened   115 g
1 teaspoon dill weed   5 ml
1 teaspoon onion powder 5 ml
1 teaspoon garlic powder 5 ml
1 tablespoon lemon juice 15 ml

- Combine all ingredients and a little pepper until they blend well. Use to saute fish or as a finishing touch.

Herb Butter for Beef

½ cup (1 stick) butter,
   softened   115 g
2 cloves garlic, minced
2 tablespoons parsley
   flakes   5 g
1½ teaspoons dried thyme 7 ml
2 tablespoons
   Worcestershire sauce   15 ml
1½ teaspoons onion powder 7 ml

- Combine all ingredients and a little pepper until they blend well.

Orange Butter

½ cup (1 stick) butter,
   softened   115 g
2 tablespoons orange
   marmalade   40 g

- Beat butter until fluffy. Add marmalade and beat until they blend well.

Potatoes

Baking Potatoes

Baking potatoes are high in starch and are good not only for baking, but for mashed potatoes and French fries. They are usually long in shape and have a coarse skin.

Russet (in various names) is the most common baking potato. (Almost all "Idaho" potatoes are russets.)

Boiling Potatoes

Boiling potatoes are relatively low in starch but high in moisture and sugar. They are sometimes referred to as waxy potatoes because of their texture. Their shapes can be long or round, and they have a smooth, thin skin.

These potatoes are good to use in soups and stews, casseroles, salads, and in any method that benefits from the fact that these potatoes hold their shape.

While they work well roasted and barbecued, they are not as desirable for mashed potatoes because they tend to be lumpy.

Some of the most common varieties include red, white, yellow, Chieftain, La Rouge, NorDonna, La Soda, Pontiac, Ruby, Sangre, and Viking.

All-purpose Potatoes

Varieties such as Allegany, Atlantic, Cascade, Castile, Chipeta, Gemchip, Irish Cobbler, Itaca, Kanona, Katahdin, Kennebec, La Chipper, Monoma, Norchip, Norwis, Onaway, Ontario, Pike, Sebago, Shepody, Snowden, Superior, White Rose and Yukon Gold can be baked, mashed and fried although they do not produce quite the same texture as baking potatoes.

They are particularly good for roasting, pan-frying, and using in soups and stews as well as in scalloped and au gratin dishes. They hold up well when boiled.

New Potatoes

A new potato is a small, immature potato of any variety. New red potatoes are the most commonly sold.

Please note: a red potato is not necessarily a new potato and a new potato is not necessarily a red potato.

Index

C

T

V